STAY OR LEAVE?

STAY OR LEAVE?

Six Steps to Resolving Your Relationship Indecision

Beverley Stone

WATKINS PUBLISHING

LONDON

This edition first published in the UK and USA 2012 by
Watkins Publishing, Sixth Floor, Castle House,
75–76 Wells Street, London W1T 3QH

1 3 5 7 9 10 8 6 4 2

Design and typesetting by Jerry Goldie Graphic Design

Printed and bound in China by Imago

British Library Cataloguing-in-Publication Data Available

Library of Congress Cataloging-in-Publication Data Available

ISBN: 978-1-78028-025-7

www.watkinspublishing.co.uk

Distributed in the USA and Canada by Sterling Publishing Co., Inc.
387 Park Avenue South, New York, NY 10016-8810

For information about custom editions, special sales, premium and
corporate purchases, please contact Sterling Special Sales
Department at 800-805-5489 or specialsales@sterlingpub.com

"So often times it happens that we live our lives
   in chains
And we never even know we have the key."[1]

Jack Tempchin and Robb Strandlund,
"Already Gone"

"I believe that courage is all too often mistakenly
seen as the absence of fear. If you descend by
rope from a cliff and are not fearful to some
degree, you are either crazy or unaware. Courage
is seeing your fear, in a realistic perspective,
defining it, considering the alternatives and
choosing to function in spite of risks."[2]

Leonard Zunin, *Contact: The First Four Minutes*

This book is for all of you who know you need to change your life, but who are struggling with your inability to decide which path to take or to act on your decision. My hope is that I can convince you that the chains that hold you back are of your own making – and that, knowing this, you will find the key to ending your relationship indecision. My intention for this book is to help you summon the courage to risk making the changes that will allow you to live a more meaningful and enjoyable life.

CONTENTS

PART III – THE SIX LIFE-CHANGING HURDLES

PREFACE

Always an "old soul", I can remember asking, "What's it all about?" from the age of three. Later, in my early teens and by then a "*lost* soul", I read extensively around the concepts of authenticity, meaning and purpose. Everything I read resonated with me. Leaving grammar school at 15, job hopping and living abroad at 17, coming back to take my A levels at 20, going to university at 21, I've always found it difficult to know "what I want to be when I grow up" – and today I'm still a "lost soul", still asking that question! But I've never found it hard to take the risk of being authentic, to find the courage to take charge of my life and to make the changes that would improve matters. These changes included leaving a difficult marriage and becoming a single parent and sole provider.

As a psychologist, I've built on my early reading to develop an approach that has helped me in my international business career. While coaching executives, I focus on helping them resolve not only their organizational dilemmas but also, more often than not, their personal ones. And it's this latter aspect of my work that led a number of people to ask me to write this book.

It all began following a conversation with Maureen Peat. She suggested that, rather than write my third book on organizational behaviour, I should capitalize on my experience as a relationship coach and write about relationships. I therefore would like to express a big debt of gratitude for her advice.

I began to write this book with fantastic help from my friend, Rachel Baird, a brilliant journalist whose writing style I love. Rachel came to my apartment in Tavira on two occasions to spend a week working with me on this book. I'm so grateful for the help she gave me in organizing my thoughts and, each time I got stuck, in helping me to express what I was trying to say accurately, succinctly and elegantly.

Then I became distracted by my research into the relationship between quantum physics and knowing, until my friend and colleague Rosemary Chesters persuaded me to revisit and finally complete this book. Rosemary felt that my message was so powerful that it would be of immense benefit to anyone with a problem in their relationship or going through the pain of indecision. I hope she's right! Rosemary agreed to my condition of completing it: that I would only do so if she'd join me at least one day a week in order to encourage, help and support me. She did so unfailingly and I thank her so much for that. There is no doubt in my mind that this book would not exist without her.

The book encompasses what I've learnt over 25 years from a diverse range of clients about their fears, challenges, relationships and group dynamics. I've consistently incorporated this learning into my thinking and practice so as to improve continuously my ability to help others, and much of what I've learnt is included in this book. My experience with clients has also enabled me to illustrate my approach with a number of case studies, although I've changed the names and some of the contexts. I therefore want to express my sincere thanks to each and every one of my clients whose willingness to persevere with my confrontational style and work with me openly, honestly and courageously is something I'll always respect and cherish.

The book would not have found its way to my publisher without the hard work and dedication of my literary agent, Susan Mears, for which I thank her. And, of course, my thanks for all her support and encouragement also go to my commissioning editor at Duncan Baird, Sandra Rigby; thanks also to my wonderfully talented editor, Fiona Robertson, who has made what could have been an arduous task into a pleasurable one, to the publicity and marketing manager, Vicky Hartley, and to the publicity and marketing executive, Fran Yarde-Buller.

Finally, I want to thank all those who generously took time to read my manuscript – my wonderful daughters, Becky Cantor and Zelda Pitman, and their lovely husbands, Joel Cantor and James Pitman; my sister-in-law and best friend, Linda Stone; my hugely supportive brother, Andrew Stone; my very special neighbour, Sandy Tyrell-Wright; and Rosemary's good friend, Jacqui Bryan. They all gave me extremely useful and hugely positive feedback that, although "Confident Me" of course agreed with them, "Cautious Me" found difficult to believe! Again, let's hope you're all correct …

INTRODUCTION

The theme of Paul Simon's popular song "50 Ways to Leave Your Lover" suggests, tongue in cheek, that the deed should be simple: you just make a new plan, Stan, slip out the back, Jack, drop off the key, Lee – and get yourself free.[1] But the singer doesn't heed his friend's repeated advice and instead doggedly remains indecisive, hesitant and in pain.

Could there be a more perfect description of what's happening to you right now? You're in a miserable relationship. You think you want to leave. Yet you are unable to do the deed. Friends, while sympathetic with "your struggle to be free", insist that the solution to your dilemma is really pretty straightforward.

When you're with them you enthusiastically get caught up in the logic of their arguments. You appreciate that they are probably right, there must be at least 50 ways to leave your lover. Yet in the morning you no longer "see the light". You are back to your old confused self, scrabbling around in the dark for clarity and certainty.

You are as baffled as everyone else by your inability to take the action that you say you hanker after: either to stay, but in a radically improved relationship, or to leave and make a new beginning. You know you're stagnating yet feel powerless to do anything about it.

Your problem may be that:

- You've been with your partner for several years but have started worrying about whether the relationship is right for you. If you are a woman, then you may be worrying about your biological clock and whether you'll be able to find someone better in time to have a baby.

- You've been married for decades and put up with an unhappy relationship for the sake of the children. Now they've left home, you are free to leave and follow the interests that your partner mocks. Yet you feel paralyzing guilt about abandoning a loyal partner just at the moment when you can start living your retirement plan.

- You're going out with someone who's messing with your mind, making you miserable and undermining your confidence. Though you know that everything your friends and family say about the destructive nature of the relationship is true, you are hooked like an addict.

- You're a married man with young children. You've met someone new, but are terrified that leaving your wife will mean missing out on time with your children.

- You're having an affair and are no longer in love with the person you live with.

- You're having an affair and are no longer in love with your extra-marital lover.

- You're living with a lovely person, but are no longer in love with or sexually attracted to him or her.

- You're in love with and sexually attracted to your partner, but he or she doesn't appear to feel the same way about you.

You are tearing yourself apart, unable to decide whether you should leave your partner or stay. This dilemma dominates your life and is constantly in your thoughts. Because you can see both sides of the argument, the never-ending swinging from go to stay and back again leaves you mentally exhausted and emotionally drained.

It is the main topic of conversation between you and your friends. You may have been on this dreadful see-saw for weeks, months or even years. But it hasn't got any easier. The conflict within you may even be making you ill.

I have seen many women and men lose a big part of themselves by staying too long in such relationships. They don't commit to staying, being their own person and making the relationship work for them. But nor do they commit to going, being their own person and making a life outside their relationship. As a result they:

- Are incredibly confused by their constant vacillation.
- Are totally obsessed by their dilemma.

3

- Know they're stagnating yet feel powerless to do anything about it.
- Become half the person they were.
- Are no longer fun to be around.
- Are suffering symptoms of stress, such as palpitations, sleeplessness, exhaustion and headaches.
- Have lost their confidence, energy and love of life.
- Can see no meaning or purpose in their life.
- Search around for help in the hope that someone else will make their decision easier.

Finding the strength to change your life can be very hard. The risks and potential repercussions seem overwhelming. The uncertainty of change is enough to put you off. Whichever choice you consider, fear and apprehension surface.

You frighten yourself with questions like: "Will I find someone better?", "How can I hurt my children and parents by leaving?", "Can I make a go of it alone?", "Is it me that's the problem?", "Do I expect too much?", "Can I cope with all the unpleasantness and disruption of moving out?", "Can I afford it?", "Do I want to go through all this again?".

So why should you even think about exposing yourself to such pain?

Because the alternative is that, by remaining the same, your life will always be as unsatisfying as it is now. And in fact, it will get worse, because you'll be increasingly angry about your own inertia or deeply depressed by the realization that the time you have to enjoy a better life is running out. The reward of finally becoming the person you want to be, of living the life you want to live, is surely worth the struggle.

I have a solution to your dilemma. It sounds simple – and it is – but it will take a lot of courage, skill and determination. The solution is to stop focusing on the detail of your relationship, stand back and take a much wider view of the rest of your time on Earth. When you take this perspective, it will be much clearer whether you are wasting your life and should move on, or whether you should work to stay with your partner. Everything in this book is about helping you to face and then work with this perspective, from the 64-Million-Dollar Questions that will encourage you to assess your life to the Six Life-Changing Hurdles that you must leap in order to take control of your future.

Even if you have spent vast sums on personal development courses, self-help books, visiting health spas, learning meditation, attending spiritual retreats or having professional counselling, and even if these activities did at first provide clarity, direction and inspiration, you just cannot seem to make the good intentions last. Such inspiration is like a drop of ink in a bath: initially a very deep, clear blue, yet within minutes it's dispersed so that you can no longer see it. Similarly, your conviction is initially very deep and clear, yet within hours, days or weeks it dissipates and you revert to muddled thinking and indecision. Time after time, even with the best of intentions, you still don't make the change.

This book is about what stops you acting on what you've learnt from all those self-help books, lengthy talks with friends, prickly discussions with your partner, spa holidays, courses and counselling sessions.

What's different about my approach, outlined in this book, is that it will show you:

- Why you can't decide whether to stay or to go.
- Why you can't stick to a decision when you do apparently "decide".
- How to take the psychological leap to stay or the physical leap to go.

You don't need me to tell you that fear is at the heart of your problem: fear of making a mistake, of making matters worse, of uncertainty. Up until now, fear has stopped you in your tracks. Unlike your previous helpers, I will not attempt to allay your fears. I will not provide comfort and reassurance. Instead, I am going to show you how to use fear to mobilize yourself.

I'm sure that you have spent many hours with people who have tried to alleviate your fears by attentively listening, clarifying, probing and "being there" for you. Yet still no change. Instead, I am going to help you to finally make your decision, and act on it, by frightening you some more. What I have to say will scare you so much that by the end of the book you will be racing to make a change!

I am going to remind you constantly about what will happen if you remain indecisive. I will confront you with the deepest fear of the human psyche – the terror of living a wasted life. You are wasting your life. And you know it. I am going to keep this thought in the front of your mind at all times, so you finally make your move.

Most likely, your previous helpers have seen their role as one of acceptance, genuineness, warmth, respect, empathy and open-mindedness. I also will be – and am – compassionate at all times. But I will not hesitate to tell it like it is! I see our relationship as both supportive and confrontational – a heroic partnership facing a world in which you are finding it hard to discover a meaningful path, and even harder to follow it.

I will help you progress by focusing on your capacity for free choice, for taking responsibility for your fate, for coping with guilt and anxiety, for finding meaning and purpose in your life, for *celebrating*, rather than fearing, being alone in the world. We will not only consider your present but also your future in terms of the choices you take to shape what you are to become. I will remind you that the path of least resistance can become a rocky road.

I will show you how to find the courage to get off the see-saw of indecision once and for all. You may finally decide to disengage from your unhappy relationship, to live an authentic life – in the sense of being true to yourself – and, by so doing, to *benefit* rather than hurt the people close to you. Or, once you have found the strength to be yourself, you may decide that you want to stay and make a go of it. Either way, your dilemma will have been resolved.

Part I – You, Now

Part I spells out how your indecision is preventing you from making the most of your one and only life. It shows how you are stagnating and making yourself ill with your indecision, and it explains that your options are either to change the situation or change the way you view it.

Part I addresses your problem with change and explains what keeps you indecisive. It provides you with the big picture – your desperate longing to live the life you are meant to live – that will help you as you progress in your struggle. This part of the book is a reality check about your current situation. It's about your aching to leave your relationship and why you're still in it. Alternatively, it's about your longing to have a better relationship and why you feel powerless to improve it. It shows how, when faced with the possibility of making a change, in reality you only have two choices in life, both equally stressful.

Part II – Your New Perspective

Part II gives you a set of 64-Million-Dollar Questions that will encourage you to hold a mirror up to yourself, challenge your current beliefs and assumptions and help you to develop a new perspective.

It will shed light on the effect that your indecision is having on you. It is a close-up view of your day-to-day life now, your struggle with yourself to be truthful and act authentically. It illustrates how you are influenced by others, by your obligations and by your commitments – and how you block yourself from changing.

These 64-Million-Dollar Questions are what you need to consider in order to live the life you want. They are your inspiration and your strategy for living an authentic life. They cover issues such as the meaning and purpose of your life; self-direction versus direction by others; being honest with yourself; values, obligations and commitments; duties to others versus duties to yourself; and tough decisions, especially those involving mutually exclusive alternatives. At the end of each chapter on the 64-Million-Dollar Questions, I've provided a short exercise that I hope will help you to integrate the key messages of each chapter into your own experience.

Chapter 10 summarizes your new perspective in terms of the Six Life-Changing Hurdles that you'll need to jump if you're to make your decision to stay or to leave and take hold of your one and only life.

Part III – The Six Life-Changing Hurdles

Part III gives you the techniques and skills that will help you overcome each of the Six Life-Changing Hurdles. These will enable you to change your thinking, feelings and behaviour in line with your new perspective.

Chapter 17, the last chapter, summarizes the whole book, giving you the keys that will release the chains that hold you back from action and freedom.

It's a tough journey

When you "decide" night after night, day after day to confront your partner, to speak frankly to your family, to leave the relationship and make a new life for yourself, or to make the radical changes that will make your existing relationship work, it's not your inability to commit to the decision that prevents action. It is, rather, that you haven't really decided. To paraphrase a Japanese proverb:

> "To decide and not to act
> is not to decide at all."

Before you moved in with your partner you may have "decided" to live together, but didn't. Then one day it just *felt right* and you did it. What about "deciding" to buy your first home together? You considered locations, looked at available property and enquired about a mortgage, but followed nothing through. Then one day, you "decide" in a very different way. Now you have a sense of urgency. You're driven to do the deed. You find the property, buy it and move in.

So what was the difference? An "apparent decision" makes rational sense and might even be appealing, but lacks a strong emotion, a gut feeling. For you to act on a decision, there needs to be congruence between what you *think* of the decision and how you *feel* about it.

After reading this book you will be indecisive no longer. The decision you make will be accompanied by a certainty that will induce change. But if you're to make your decision, and act upon it, you will need to commit yourself to a tough journey because:

- It's tough to be free.
- It's tough to make decisions.
- It's tough to act on decisions.
- It's tough to choose.
- It's tough to be responsible for your actions and for your failures to act.
- It's tough to travel alone.
- It's tough to fight to be yourself.

As the poet e.e. cummings puts it, our biggest challenge in life is to be nobody but ourselves in a world that's trying its hardest to make us everybody else.[2]

It's a tough journey. But I hope that this book helps you take the first step in deciding to be nobody but yourself and convinces you that it's well worth the ride.

PART I

YOU, NOW

CHAPTER 1

SO YOUR INDECISION IS FINAL?

Your reasons to go

I don't know why you want to leave your lover. It may be because your partner is:

- Now a good friend but nothing more
- Emotionally or physically not there for you
- Damaging your confidence, sanity and health through psychological or physical abuse
- Not quite right
- Not right
- Holding values and attitudes that are no longer compatible with yours
- Unacceptably antisocial and/or rude to family and friends
- No longer the one you love – there's someone else
- No longer the one you love – there's someone else who's a possibility.

Your reasons to stay

And you may want to stay because:

- You don't want to hurt or disrupt your children or your partner.
- You think your partner's got potential.
- Your partner's lovely some of the time.
- You're worried about coping financially without your partner.
- You don't want to waste the time and energy you've put into the relationship.
- Everyone likes your partner and you're worried they'll disapprove if you leave.
- You fear being alone.
- You fear being alone *for ever*.
- You've invested in a house and possessions together and the upheaval is unthinkable.

Whatever your reasons, the problem is the same. You keep vacillating between leaving and staying.

You're confused by your inability to act

You've thought about leaving, talked about it with your partner, friends, family, life coach or counsellor. You've convinced yourself that you need to make a change. You know that you either have to change your attitude toward the situation or your behaviour toward each other, or you have to make a physical move out of your relationship and house. You've even planned how and when you will make the change.

Yet somehow, when you arrive back home or meet your partner again, your resolution always fades. Each and every time you fall back into old patterns of behaviour and stay stuck in the same situation. And you repeat this process many, many times. You are as confused by your inability to take action as everyone else.

You have probably applied varied techniques to your problem. You and your friends may have tried being logical by analyzing the positive and negative aspects of your partner's character and the pros and cons of separating or staying. Together, you may have worked through self-help books to identify your strengths, goals, values and ideals. If you have consulted a life coach you will most likely have used traditional problem-solving skills to:

- Brainstorm choices
- Select options
- Write a personal vision
- Calculate likely outcomes
- Set priorities
- Establish clear goals
- Create a realistic action plan
- Determine the next step
- Set yourself deadlines.

And you may well have acknowledged, and learnt how to overcome, self-defeating problems such as fear and anxiety, low self-esteem or telling yourself that the timing's not right. Yet, still no change. You may have gone to professional relationship counselling for help, where you and your counsellor hoped that by having more, and more open, conversations exploring problems and solutions, you would stumble, if only through the "process of fatigue", on the perfect way forward – and spring into action. But you didn't. You haven't. You don't.

However sound the conclusions of so very many such conversations seem at the time and however honest your resolve to choose one path or the other, each time you leave a conversation, you find yourself back in the loop, raking over excellent reasons to stay and ever better reasons to leave.

You're stagnating yet feel powerless to do anything about it

By going over and over the same ground, making an apparent decision and yet not taking the action that would change your life for the better, you may identify with the characters in Samuel Beckett's play *Waiting for Godot*. They too reflect, plan, resolve and procrastinate, but never act. The play ends with the following:

> "Estragon: Well, shall we go?
>
> Vladimir: Yes, let's go.
>
> *Stage direction: They do not move.*"[1]

Jennie is a great example of this. She is living with her hyper-critical partner, Stephen, who undermines her confidence and is antisocial. Most of the time she is really unhappy. Yet on occasion Jennie and Stephen get on so well together that she feels like he's her soulmate and loves being with him. When Stephen is being cruel, Jennie threatens in numerous conversations with her girl-friends to leave him by "next month" if things don't improve. Her friends unfailingly agree that he is bad for her and that she should without doubt leave him and that they will happily help her move out.

But another month passes, Stephen doesn't change – and Jennie doesn't leave. She feels embarrassed to see her friends, as they are flabbergasted by her inability to free herself from a damaging relationship. Yet, equally, she feels powerless to unhook from Stephen's hold over her.

So for Jennie, and her friends, it's "Shall we go? Let's go. No one moves."

Do you recognize yourself in those three lines? Doesn't this example of abortive decision-making sum up what's happening to you when, day after day, you struggle with your decision to stay or leave your relationship? You dissect your situation, weigh up the alternatives, choose a solution and make an apparent decision, but when it comes to the crunch, you remain where you are and carry on as before. In effect, "no one moves."

You've lost yourself and it's making you ill

And so you go back over and over the same ground with the same people who, though supportive, patient and there for you are, you suspect, in reality, on hearing your voice at the end of a phone or seeing you at the door, starting to lose the will to live! In fairness, so are you. You are as bored and exhausted by the whole situation as they are.

And not only that. If your inability to make a decision has lasted for months or even years, your continued languishing in a problematic relationship will have begun to affect who you are. It will be diminishing you. You will have lost your sparkle, your wit, your confidence. You are generally unhappy and it's making you ill. You may have begun to suffer symptoms of stress such as migraines, IBS, indigestion, eczema, sleeplessness, oversleeping, loss of appetite, overeating or increased alcohol consumption.

Your indecisiveness can also impact on your work and career. You may be unfocused, disorganized and disengaged. If you have children your preoccupation will have an effect not only on the quality but also the quantity of your interactions with them. Your vacillation will also limit your social life and undermine your friendships. People are less likely to invite you to social events – this week you're a couple, next week you're not and they get frustrated by constant changes to their plans. Additionally, they, and you, are tired of your relationship being the main topic of conversation and of you as a person being totally eclipsed by your obsession with dissecting your partner's character and deliberating over the "big decision".

It's time to change

Your dilemma is something that never goes away; it is always on your mind. Well, not any more! It's time to make a move. These are your three options right now:

1. Stay and change the situation – do whatever it takes to make your relationship one that you'll enjoy.

2. Leave and change the situation – start a new life, one that will be more rewarding.

3. Stay and view your situation differently – remain but change the way you perceive your partner, yourself and your situation.

You must either change the situation or change the way you view it. What you can no longer do is choose to carry on living in the same situation and view it with horror and distaste. This is just a dreadful drain on your energy, a pointless waste of your life and it's making you ill.

In the next chapter, I'm going to explain how and why we avoid change, and the impact that this has on our chances of having a fulfilled and happy life.

CHAPTER 2

WHY NO CHANGE?

Being authentic

Why is it so difficult for you to make the change? Because choosing one thing means that you exclude something else. The fear of leaving behind what you have makes you convince yourself that it's not that bad. But it is. You are wasting your life with such self-talk. You are either in a bad relationship and not doing what it takes to improve it, or you are in a rotten relationship and not doing what it takes to move out and move on with someone more compatible. So how do you go forward and leave behind what in truth you no longer want?

When you are desperate to make a change, it is a crunch moment in your life. And what crunch moments have in common is the opportunity to live your values and be the person you are meant to be – to be authentic. To do this at will, whenever an opportunity arises, you need to have a philosophy that provides you with the courage to act *now* – as Nike puts it, "Just do it!" Model 1, showing how we learn and thereby change, is useful in this respect.

This model shows how we often stagnate in an endless triangle of doing, reflecting and planning. Currently you are *doing* something you are not happy about – being in an inadequate relationship. You spend a great deal of your time at work, lunch, driving home, during the evening, in the middle of the night *reflecting* on your situation – your frustrations and your fear of wasting time. You are constantly *planning* to make a change – either to confront your partner, make some mutually agreed permanent improvements and stay, or to end the relationship and go your own ways.

Crossing your Rubicon

Had you taken the next step you would now be *experimenting* with your plan, one way or the other. You would be crossing your own, personal Rubicon*. By that I mean committing to *act* upon your decision, go through the "point of no return" and leave your indecision behind.

But what you are doing instead is stopping yourself becoming everything you could be. When it comes to the crunch, you don't dare experiment. Instead you spend your life going round and round the triangle of doing, reflecting and planning.

---

* Crossing the Rubicon is a proverbial phrase meaning to go past the point of no return. The Rubicon river was a boundary between Cisalpine Gaul and Roman Italy. In 49 BCE Julius Caesar crossed it as a deliberate act of war. The historian Suetonius quoted Caesar as having said "The die is cast" upon taking this action.

Model 1: Triangulating – how you stagnate

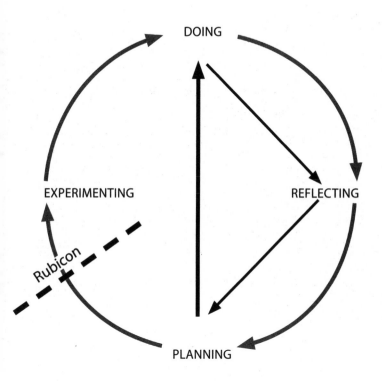

Triangulating – how you stagnate

You reflect on your relationship, life and future; you make ambitious plans to change; yet when it comes down to it, you do nothing:

- You think about (reflect on) moving out, plan to do it, but don't.
- You think about seeing a solicitor to assess your position, plan to do it, but don't.
- You think about confronting your partner about his or her behaviour, plan to do it, but don't.
- You think about challenging your partner more skilfully, plan to do it, but don't.
- You think about focusing on your partner's good qualities while ignoring irritating habits, plan to do it, but don't.
- You think about resigning yourself to a life of mediocrity, thereby ending your craving to go, plan to do it, but don't.
- You think about standing up to disapproving parents and friends, plan to do it, but don't.
- You think about broaching the subject with your children, plan to do it, but don't.
- You think about really doing it this time, plan to do it, but don't.

The triangulating model is also true of many people's lives more generally. People spend weeks, months and even years going around the triangle, reflecting on what they're doing in terms of their behaviour, situation or life, making ambitious plans to change but, when it comes to the crunch, doing nothing. Maybe you recognize yourself in some of these aborted "decisions", too:

- You think about asking for promotion at work, plan to do it, but don't.
- You think about making a new life abroad, plan to do it, but don't.
- You think about starting your own business, plan to do it, but don't.
- You think about writing the book, plan to do it, but don't.
- You think about doing something more meaningful with your life, plan to do it, but don't.
- You think about asking a difficult work colleague to be more cooperative, plan to do it, but don't.

You do not act on your hopes and dreams. From the trivial to the life changing, you never cross Rubicons and experiment with your plans. No wonder at times you feel desperate, restless and trapped.

The problem with change

Why don't we cross the Rubicon, even though we're unhappy? Why don't we follow through our plan to either stay or leave? Why would we rather vacillate than take the risk of saying what we mean and doing what we say? As I said at the start of this chapter, fear is the answer.

How does it feel, crossing Rubicons? How does the thought of moving out, seeing a solicitor, confronting our partner, changing our style, being less demanding, accepting mediocrity, standing up to a disapproving parent or telling our children, feel? Yes, scary. The very thought of it makes us anxious. Butterflies in the stomach, increased heart rate, dry mouth and so on.

The huge and obvious risk associated with the uncertainty of leaving creates such fearful thoughts as:

- "What will my life be like without my partner – will it be better or worse?"
- "Will I be able to cope with the break-up and all that it involves in terms of selling the house, changing bank accounts, furniture removal, the children's sanity, emotional upheaval, the arguments with my partner and disapproval of parents and of friends?"
- "What if I can't find anyone better?"

Equally, the huge and obvious risk associated with the uncertainty of staying creates such fearful thoughts as:

- "What if I'm stuck with *this* for the rest of my life!"
- "If I did leave, I could do better."
- "Why am I putting up with someone that I wouldn't wish on anyone else? Do I think that little of myself?"
- "Is staying together better for our children or worse?"

So the fear that stops us crossing Rubicons is fear of:

- Getting it wrong
- Upsetting others or incurring their disapproval
- The unknown.

You fear the unknown because, from this side of your Rubicon, you cannot tell whether or not crossing it will be a mistake. You don't know whether you'll:

- Be happier or even more miserable
- Be a hero or a villain
- Be better or worse off
- Succeed or fail
- Be popular or ostracized
- Make the right or wrong choice
- Be more fulfilled or less.

But how does it feel right now?

Now I'm going to frighten you into making a move.

For all the above reasons, crossing your Rubicon is stressful – that's true. But how does it feel standing still in life? How does it feel right now, not taking the risk, keeping your head down, playing it safe, finding yourself in the same position week after week?

How does it feel at three o'clock in the morning, lying in bed, when your eyes flash open, your heart is pounding and your mind is once again racing with thoughts about how miserable and unsatisfying your life is?

Yes, that's right – stressful!

You only have two choices in life

You imagine that, by standing still, you can avoid the stress and anxiety that you associate with initiating a change. Yet, in reality, life is stressful either way. A crucial step in overcoming your indecision is to realize that you have just *two choices in life*:

Choice 1

To suffer the guilt and STRESS of standing still, keeping your head down, playing it safe, staying in an unsatisfactory relationship, knowing that you are neither happy nor fulfilling your life's ambitions, only to regret your lost opportunities later in life. You already, and will always, suffer the stress associated with the guilt of looking back on an inauthentic, wasted life and saying, "If only I had …".

Choice 2

To suffer the anxiety and STRESS associated with jumping into the abyss of uncertainty and taking the risk of being happier and more fulfilled by making a decision, standing firm and acting on it once and for all. Only by repeatedly crossing your Rubicons in this way can you learn, develop and fulfil your life's potential.

You can't escape stress – so stop trying

I cannot emphasize enough that there is no escape in life from either the stress associated with the guilt of standing still or the stress that accompanies the uncertainty of experimenting with change.

Either choice is risky, but taking the risk of making your decision and crossing your Rubicon offers you the chance of a life you can look back on with contentment and pride.

In the words of the 17th-century Hasidic rabbi, Susya, on his deathbed:

"When I get to heaven they will not ask me
'Why were you not Moses?'

Instead they will ask 'Why were you not Susya?

Why did you not become what only you could have become?'"

If you're to become what only you could become, in effect there *is* no choice! You *must* cross your Rubicon.

CHAPTER 3

WILL EITHER DECISION REALLY END IN CATASTROPHE?

Catastrophic fantasies don't help

We've seen how crossing Rubicons is inevitably stressful, because we don't know what we'll need to deal with on the other side. But we make it worse for ourselves. We avoid crossing our Rubicons because of what I call catastrophic fantasies.

Our catastrophic fantasies are catastrophic because we always think the worst ("I will never meet anyone again"; "I can't cope alone") and fantasies because they rarely happen. Chances are, if you take the risk, you will meet someone else and be far happier; you can and will cope on your own and very likely enjoy the peace and simplicity of it all! Catastrophic fantasies often arise from the fear of hurting people or of invoking their disapproval. Consequently, we hold ourselves back rather than take the risk of being honest.

David could not tell his parents that he wanted to marry a woman of a different religion, Jessica, for fear that it would "kill them" and that they'd reject him for ever. Instead, he chose to live secretly with Jessica, with only his friends knowing. He denied Jessica and himself children, as that would have been too much of a lie to live with. Every so often, David was tempted to tell his parents, but the thought of their reaction always prevented him. Finally, after his mother's death and when he was well into his 50s, he owned up to his father.

His father's reaction both stunned and devastated David and Jessica. His father was thrilled that he had found someone to love and said that his mother would have been thrilled, too. All she had worried about and prayed for was that her son would find a good woman who loved him and could have his children – her grandchildren. What a waste of life. And all because David imagined catastrophe.

This is a gross example of how the fear created by catastrophic fantasies stops people from being authentic and crossing their Rubicons. They spend nights, days and weeks worrying, when most of the time their worries are unfounded. How often have you suffered a tense evening and disturbed night fretting about the next day at home or work and, in the event, nothing bad happened? In the words of the 19th-century American humourist Mark Twain:

> "I have known a great many troubles, but most of them never happened."

Overcoming catastrophic fantasies and either leaving for pastures new or demanding new ground-rules as a prerequisite for staying, can be dangerous. But the model "Triangulating – how you stagnate" reminds us that so, too, can living an inauthentic, unfulfilled life.

Change is a learning experience

In addition, it should be said that, for me, crossing a Rubicon *doesn't* mean that you can never go back. You can cross your Rubicon and choose to return. People do. People:

- Break up with their partner, have a few "flings" and then get back together with their partner permanently.
- Remarry those they divorce.
- Return to organizations they've left.
- Emigrate to the other side of the world, then decide to return.

Imad felt suffocated by his marriage to Thuraya and by his two small daughters. He longed for the life he had before he married, when he spent his income on himself – clothes, nightclubs, women, holidays, computer games, the latest technological gadgets and so on.

After numerous arguments and much soul-searching, he left Thuraya and the children and returned to his old lifestyle. He had the children every other weekend. Thuraya meanwhile chose to behave in a reasonable, non-confrontational manner throughout, hoping to remain friends for the sake of their children.

After nine months of his bachelor lifestyle, Imad saw a pointless life stretching before him and longed for the mean-ingfulness of the loving family that he'd left. He asked Thuraya to take him back, which she did. Having had the fling he thought he wanted, he learnt that in reality he valued everything he'd already had.

The difference between those people who cross their Rubicon and those who do not, is that the former accept the risk of making a mistake. By experimenting with their dream and *learning* from their experience, they ensure that they can never look back and regret not having followed their heart, not having lived their dream.

To paraphrase George Bernard Shaw: when you are lying on your deathbed looking back on your life it's not the things that you did that you'll regret, it's the things you didn't do.

You won't be lying on your deathbed cringing about your embarrassing behaviour, say, at a dinner party last Saturday. Rather, if you've succumbed to your catastrophic fantasies, you'll be asking yourself: "Why didn't I leave my partner in time to make a better life?" or "Why couldn't I have been big enough to focus on the good and ignore the bad?" or "Why didn't I just get on with my life and start my own business?" or "Why couldn't I have stopped my workaholic lifestyle to spend more time with my family?"

Looking back from your deathbed at 94, the idea of moving out and starting again 30, 40, 50 years earlier, or asking the person you're living with either to do what they promise and work with you to improve the relationship, or admit they never will and help you end it, will seem a trivial and obvious Rubicon to cross. In the whole scheme of things, is your decision so difficult to make and are the obstacles really so difficult to overcome?

Are you sitting in the waiting room of life?

Franz Kafka's novel *The Trial* is about a man who is accused of wasting his life. He fails to take chances that would have led him to become the person he could have been. Instead, he timidly waits for others to give him permission to do so, and as a result his life is largely futile. In the book, Kafka relates the following parable that says it all:

> "Before the law* stands a doorkeeper. A man from the country comes to this doorkeeper and asks to be admitted to the law. But the doorkeeper tells him he cannot grant him admittance to the law now. The man considers this, and asks whether he can be admitted later. 'It is possible,' says the doorkeeper, 'but not now.'

---

* There are myriad connotations of the word law used by Kafka beyond its simple juridical meaning. It may also mean the law of God, or of nature, or the institutionalized law of the state.

Since the door to the law is standing open as it always does, the man stoops to look inside through the door as the doorkeeper steps to one side. When the doorkeeper sees this he laughs and says: 'If you are so keen, try to get in against my orders. But take note of this: I am powerful, and I am only the lowest doorkeeper. But in one hall after another there are more doorkeepers, each more powerful than the last. Even I cannot bear to look at the third one.'

The man from the country did not expect such difficulties ... he decides he would rather wait until he gets permission to enter. The doorkeeper gives him a stool and lets him sit down to one side of the door. He sits there for days and years. ... He curses his unhappy fate, in the first years out loud, but later, when he is old, he only mutters to himself. He becomes childish ... .

In the end his eyesight grows weak, and he cannot tell whether it is really getting darker around him or whether his eyes are deceiving him. But he does now notice an inextinguishable radiance that streams from the entrance to the law. By now he does not have very long to live. Before he dies, everything that he has experienced during all this time focuses in his mind into one question that he has not asked the doorkeeper before. He beckons him, for he can no longer lift his stiffening body. The doorkeeper has to bend low to hear him, for the difference in their height has increased, much to the disadvantage of the man.

'What is it you want to know now?' says the doorkeeper. 'You are insatiable.'

'Everyone aspires to the law,' says the man, 'so how is it that in all these years no one except me has demanded admittance?'

The doorkeeper realizes that the man is finished, and so that the dying man's ears can catch his words, he roars at him: 'No one else could be admitted here, this door was meant only for you. Now I am going to shut it.'"[1]

What are we to make of this chilling tale? Kafka's man was guilty of living an unlived life, of succumbing to his fears, of waiting for the permission from others to make his move, of not seizing his life. As a result, he died "like a dog", malingering in the waiting room of life. He never became even half the man he could have been had he found the courage to go through doors that were intended for him alone.

Are you guilty of living an unlived life?

Are you in the waiting room of life, succumbing to your fears? Are you in danger of never becoming half the person you could be? You can no longer sit and wait for it to feel safe to make your move. It never will and, by hoping against hope, you are already beginning to regret a wasted life.

You don't want words like these on your tombstone, do you?:

— ❦ —

BORN 1976

DIED 2012

BURIED 2070

— ❦ —

Don't die malingering. Seize your life. *Now* is the time to go through those doors intended for you alone.

STOP REVVING YOUR ENGINE WITH YOUR FOOT ON THE BRAKE

"It's not that bad"

Now at this point you may be saying to yourself, "Beverley's painting a horrific picture of stagnation and waste of life, but it's not that bad." Well that may be true and, if it's not that bad, focus on the great stuff and stop thinking about the bad or average stuff. Commit to stay, view the situation differently and make a go of it. I believe in the concept of "readiness"; if you truly mean that it's not that bad, then OK, you're not yet ready.

But are you actually one of those people who say "it's not that bad" when confronted with your unwillingness to cross your Rubicon, yet don't mean it? Allen Wheelis uses the following metaphor to describe those who feel unable to make a decision:

"Some persons sit at the crossroads, taking
neither path because they cannot take
both, cherishing the illusion that if they
sit there long enough, the two ways will
resolve themselves into one and hence both
be possible." [1]

Sitting at the crossroads, taking neither path because they cannot take both, is something most people can identify with at some point in their lives. This is what's happening when you go through the motions of your relationship so that you're not really in it, yet don't leave it to make a go of another one. You can neither decide to say "Yes" nor to say "No".

You may fool yourself that it's not that bad – a bit like sitting in the sun, eating a picnic on the grass at a leafy countryside crossroads while you decide which path to take next. You endlessly weigh up the pros and cons, deciding which way to jump, yet remain hovering in limbo.

It *is* that bad

But those of you who are at the crossroads, really wishing you could change, in all honesty know that it's a lot worse than hovering in limbo. A better metaphor for not crossing your Rubicon is that of a aeroplane that must take off from a very short runway.

In order to get up the impetus to fly, the pilot must rev the engine while keeping one foot firmly on the brake. When the engine is whirring, the whole plane shakes, throbs and strains at the brakes, and would eventually destroy itself if it did not take off and fly. Revving the engine with the brakes on would be completely senseless without the clear intention, when the right moment came, of releasing the brakes and taking off.

Imagine you are that plane. Caught in indecision, you experience it straining forward while the brake is still on. And if you rev your engine for some time, you will eventually shake yourself to pieces.

You are not merely hovering in harmless limbo. You are tearing yourself apart. You are not idling in neutral but are rather in a situation of extreme conflict – the conflict between not moving and moving. You are continually wrestling with your internal struggle, your agonizing decision.

So it *is* that bad for many of you, because through your unwillingness to change your situation, you yourself have changed – and probably for the worse. Many of you have become half the person you were.

When I first met Jon, he'd spent several years torturing himself over whether to leave his partner, Anna. She undermined his confidence by finding fault with everything he did. She was confrontational during arguments and so Jon learnt to give in, and no longer fought his corner.

Anna's constant demonstration of her contempt for Jon impacted on his work. He lost his confidence and began to allow certain members of his team to treat him, as Anna did, with disdain. As a result, the quality of his team's work diminished along with his department's reputation. For the first time in his life, Jon's boss was critical of his work and leadership. He was now unable to recognize himself either at home or at work.

Whenever he had a spare moment alone, he fretted over how he had lost his dynamism, confidence and popularity. He recognized that Anna's behaviour toward him was behind his problem, as did his friends, yet he felt compelled to stay with her. Each time he "decided" to move out, the disruption of leaving felt worse than the misery of staying.

By not leaving Anna, which in his heart he knew he wanted to do, he held himself back with his foot on the brake and so had chosen to tear himself apart.

PART II
YOUR NEW PERSPECTIVE

CHAPTER 5

YOUR NEW PERSPECTIVE

A new approach to your dilemma

You may balk at my suggestion at the end of the previous chapter, that Jon had "chosen" to tear himself apart.

The problem is that most people convince themselves that they don't have any choices in life. You may have lulled yourself into believing that, because your world is full of commitments and obligations, you do not have the freedom to choose to break away.

Or that no one would take the risk of rocking the boat by speaking their minds in a family that appears on the surface to be muddling along nicely.

Or you may say that no one would be courageous enough to stay and demand change with a partner as aggressive as yours. Or insensitive enough to expect change from a partner as ill equipped.

In other words, you may well feel that you:

- Have no choice but to live your life for everyone else
- Feel trapped and
- Blame others for it!

Whereas, if you're to live meaningfully and authentically, you need to accept that, in reality, you are in the situation you find yourself because you have:

- Made choices
- Freely, and are therefore
- Responsible for your predicament.

The 64-Million-Dollar Questions

The idea contained in these three statements may be difficult for you to accept right now.

Asking yourself all the 64-Million-Dollar Questions posed in the next four chapters will help you realize the truth of these three propositions.

The 64-Million-Dollar Questions will give you new ways of understanding your current dilemma, help you to internalize your new perspective and encourage you to finally change your life.

THE 64-MILLION-DOLLAR QUESTIONS:

Accepting responsibility for your impasse

QUESTION 1

....

Who are you trying to please?

Many people find it difficult to make changes to their lives because, in worrying about what others will think, they blame them for their own behaviour. Clients say to me, "I'm miserable as sin, I hate my life, but I can't do anything about it."

So I ask, "Why not? Who are you trying to please?" and they reply, "My parents", "My children", "My partner", "My friends", "My community." They feel powerless to do what matters to them and, therefore, are neither being authentic nor living a meaningful life. No wonder, then, that they become depressed, stressed and ill.

Why do we try to please everyone but ourselves? As children, we are encouraged to believe that others know best, especially at school and often at home. We are taught that there's a right and wrong, and as we grow up we are made to look foolish (by parents, teachers, bosses, religious leaders and so on) if we don't abide by this perception – the perception of those in authority. Conversely, if we do abide by it, we are given approval.

As a result, we develop an impression that there is always a "right" answer, that other people have it, and that if we can conform and "get it right", we will win their approval. We grow up with the idea that there is a perfect way to behave and that making mistakes is terrible because we will no longer seem perfect and people will not love us unless we are. This idea results in the repression of any of our own views, beliefs, needs and wants that may go against the people we care about and hence cause their disapproval.

If, as an adult, you continue trying to please other people or gain their approval by living by their values and opinions, meeting their needs and wants while suppressing your own, you have only yourself to blame. You can't blame others for feeling trapped. As the Japanese author D.T. Suzuki puts it in his *Manual of Zen Buddhism*:

> "Thus, when they ask
>> 'How can I ever get emancipated?',
>
> ₁ the Zen Master may answer:
>> 'Who has ever put you in bondage?'"[1]

I am not advocating that you be cruel or thoughtless and not try to please others or put their feelings first *sometimes*. I am simply saying that no one has "put you in bondage"; you are free to do anything you like. And on this occasion, you must decide whether or not you're going to live your life according to your *own* values, those that define what's right and wrong for *you*.

QUESTION 2

....

Are you your own jailor?

Clients also tell me they feel trapped by their social and financial obligations. They blame their inability to make a change on such responsibilities as contributing to a joint mortgage, having to earn a hefty salary to maintain their family's lifestyle, or not disrupting their children's education and friendships by making them move schools.

They say, "I'm wavering because every time I make a firm decision, I worry about the news damaging my parents' health", or "I can't do it because it devastates me to think of my children feeling torn between the two of us", or "My community has been so supportive and everyone assumes we're doing fine. If they blame me for the break-up, I'm scared they'll disown me."

Whenever you waiver, do you feel equally immobilized by your obligations? Do you fear that moving out will mean a longer commute to work that will reduce your time with your children and impact their self-confidence? Do you worry that a divorce might embarrass your parents? Are you anxious that you can't exist without your partner's income? Do you feel guilty that your partner, who has a physical disability, relies on you for care? Or maybe you cannot contemplate adding the inevitable arguments and unpleasantness to your already stressful life?

Alternatively, do you use commitments as your excuse for not making the move *today*: your daughter came to stay for the weekend; your partner made an effort this week; it's your partner's birthday soon and it wouldn't be fair? Perhaps you've booked a holiday together and feel you can't un-book it. Or you're both invited to a wedding and it would be embarrassing not to go. Maybe one of you is incapacitated with 'flu and needs looking after.

Whenever clients feel imprisoned by their obligations, I relate Hubert Benoit's description of a man who similarly imagines himself to be a prisoner, trapped in a small, dark cell. Standing on his toes, he grasps the bars of a tiny window, the only apparent source of light. If he holds on tight, straining upward, he can see a bit of bright sunlight between the top bars. He is so focused on not losing sight of this glimmer of hope-giving light that it never occurs to him to let go and explore the rest of the cell. As a result, he never discovers that the door at the end of the cell is open; that he is, in fact, free. He has always been free to walk out into the brightness of day, if only he would let go.[2] As Sheldon Kopp put it:

> "[In life] we are defeated not only by the
> narrowness of our perspective, and our fear
> of the darkness, but by our excuses as well …
> we make circumstances our prison and other
> people our jailors."[3]

Ziggy had for years been clinging on to his dream of leaving his job and becoming a playwright – his "glimmer of hope-giving light". He convinced himself, however, that his obligations to his wife, Linda, and son, Sam, prevented him from living this dream. He therefore felt himself to be a prisoner, trapped in a dark cell with no hope of escape.

After a number of sessions, Ziggy accepted that he could either choose to carry on making circumstances his excuse and people his jailors, and live a life of regret, or choose to use his potential. He chose to broaden his perspective on making the most of his time on earth, convinced his wife of his commitment to success as a playwright and thereby freed himself to take the risk of crossing his Rubicon.

Are you making circumstances your prison and other people your jailors? In reality, like Ziggy and Benoit's man, you are your own jailor. You may say, as do my clients, "How can I possibly be responsible for not crossing my Rubicon when I've just told you I can't because of my social and financial obligations?"

Well, you're not responsible if you define "responsibility" as follows:

> "Responsibility, n. A detachable burden easily shifted to the shoulders of God, Fate, Fortune, Luck or one's neighbour.
>
> In the days of astrology it was customary to unload it upon a star."[4]

....

Who's pulling your strings?

But for me, responsibility is by no means a "detachable burden". This is because, when I speak of your responsibility, I am not merely talking about your responsibility for your behaviour in crossing or not crossing your Rubicon. I am talking about your responsibility for *being yourself*. Once we're here, on this planet, what we make of ourselves is up to us. It's our responsibility and ours alone.

So if you want either to go for good or stay with radical changes, yet you are choosing neither path and instead blaming obligations and other people then, yes, you are responsible.

- You are responsible for *choosing* to be passive.
- You are responsible for *choosing* to put obligations and commitments first.
- You are responsible for *choosing* not to take control of your one and only life.
- You are responsible for *choosing* instead to live a life that is a sham.
- You are responsible for *choosing* to continue to be degraded.
- You are responsible for *choosing* to suffer the consequences of your own inaction.

Responsibility in this sense is inseparable from freedom – the freedom to choose. In choosing what you are to become, you have absolute freedom; even refusing to choose represents a choice.

In the words of the existential psychotherapist Irving Yalom:

> "One is … entirely responsible for one's life,
> not only for one's actions but for one's *failures*
> to act." [5]

Every day you choose what you are going to do or not do, say or not say, eat or not eat, what goals you will pursue or forgo, who you will put first or last, what you will continue with or change. So, I'm afraid that you *are* responsible for creating your own suffering, your own situation and your own destiny. And so yes, like Jon at the end of Chapter 4, you are responsible for tearing yourself apart.

Granted you may be choosing one thing over another to avoid the consequences of an unpopular or uncomfortable decision. But the fact is, no one is pulling your strings. You are not a puppet. If you are to stop tearing yourself apart and live life to the full, you must acknowledge that you are freely choosing to do with your life what you are now doing – vacillating. And that, equally, you could freely choose to do a number of other things: go for good; stay and make improvements; move out yet continue to be a couple; divorce; have a trial separation – whatever.

Self-reflection

Try completing the following sentences:

1. I am responsible for feeling trapped by trying to please

....

....

....

Example: *I am responsible for feeling trapped by trying to please my parents.*

2. I am responsible for choosing to ....

....

....

....

Example: *I am responsible for choosing to live a life that is a sham.*

3. I could equally accept the consequences of my choice
   and choose instead to......................................

....

....

....

Example: *I could equally accept the consequences of my choice and choose instead to tell my parents and deal with the fallout.*

THE 64-MILLION-DOLLAR QUESTIONS:

Accepting the downside of your decision

....

What are you waiting for?

Even if you accept responsibility for your situation, you may find that your feet remain firmly rooted to the spot. Awareness of your sole responsibility for your indecision is not synonymous with change. You have only reached the threshold of change and need to move beyond awareness to decision and action.

One reason why you continue to struggle and sit at your crossroads is that, whenever you decide to do one thing, you are met head on with the fact that you will have to give up something else. This is the implication of your choice: for every "yes" there must be a "no".

Social and financial "baggage", for example, can equally be viewed positively as advantages – the large house, the status car, membership of a golf club, expensive seats at the theatre, private education for the children, a personal trainer, the social "set". Not making your move could simply be your reaction to wanting to maintain advantages like these.

Even if you see the possibility of recreating yourself through decisive action, you may fear letting go of all the privileges and people that provide your security, lifestyle and self-concept. So, although I may sometimes sound harsh, I do empathize that the hardest thing about changing your life is letting go of your options, knowing they may never come again.

Julia was married to a titled banker, James, lived in a beautiful home on a private estate and enjoyed a full social life and the status that went with her title. However, before her marriage she had been a partner in a successful law firm and she felt that her identity had become overshadowed by James's reputation as a well-known CEO. Julia came to me because she was finding it harder and harder to play the supportive wife, feeling invisible and disrespected by James's colleagues at the functions she regularly attended to help his career. She told me that she wanted to resume her career, but that when she discussed this with James he was adamant that he needed her to remain the supportive housewife; that there wasn't room for both of them to be preoccupied by a career.

So Julia began to feel as invisible and disrespected at home as at functions. By the time we met, she was having a great deal of difficulty trying to choose between all her current advantages and taking the risk of going it alone. Eventually, she chose to go it alone and learn to live happily with the downside of her decision – the loss of the financial and social trappings of her previous situation – and enjoy the upside of regaining her authentic self.

Decisions, then, are painful because they remind us that life consists of a limited number of possibilities. We attempt to avoid this awareness by avoiding decisions. To overcome this avoidance, I ask clients, "What are you waiting for?" and they reply, "Well, what will happen if I cross my Rubicon and I've made a big mistake? I'm frightened I'll regret it."

In answer to this I suggest that they keep in mind one of the characters in *Either/Or*, by the 19th-century philosopher Kierkegaard. This character believes that – either/or – it doesn't matter what you choose, chances are you will always regret your choice! "If you marry, you will regret it. If you do not marry, you will regret it."

If you stay single then you may regret going through life unable to share your experiences, yet if you find a partner then you may regret the lost peace and quiet and autonomy of being single. If you procrastinate and wait for the two paths to become one (which won't, of course, happen), what will you achieve with your life? Although we may regret our decision we need to remember that we regret our indecision, too.

QUESTION 5

....

Are you avoiding responsibility for the years already wasted?

Maybe you aren't making the change, even though you accept responsibility for your predicament, because making the change now would mean that you could have made it long ago.

If you accept that you can decide to change your life now, then you must accept that you have always been capable of taking that decision. By refusing to choose to change, you attempt to avoid accepting your guilt for the damage you have already done to yourself in living a life of untapped possibilities.

Recently, I suggested to a client of mine, Libby, that she take a six-month break from her affair with a married man, Stephen, to whom she was addicted, but who was damaging her mental health. Without hesitation, Libby responded by saying that she couldn't – because it would mean that she was responsible for wasting the past 10 years with him. If she unhooked from him now, she would be confronted by the fact that she could have unhooked from him a year ago, five years ago or more.

Please keep in the front of your mind the idea that avoiding the present decision, in order to avoid the guilt of past decisions, merely perpetuates the situation. You cannot undo or atone for the past, other than by deciding to change your present and your future.

QUESTION 6

....

Are you hoping someone will hold your hand?

Another problem with making your decision, even though you accept personal responsibility, is that taking action can shift you from your everyday experience to one where you see yourself objectively, as a being that is totally alone in the world. Sometimes, this shift in perspective can be a liberating experience while at other times it is a very threatening one. When it feels threatening, you avoid the experience by avoiding a decision.

When you're with friends, a counsellor, in workshops or with relatives you feel empowered, decisive and ready for action. But as soon as you're alone once more, the cost of the decision – arguments, loneliness, uncertainty, anxiety, failure, poverty, hardship, heartache, having to find the strength and courage – confronts you with the fact that, though the support of others may be great, fundamentally you'll be crossing this Rubicon alone. Fear overwhelms you and you begin once more to question what you really want. Your resolve dissipates and you can no longer summon the will-power to act.

A decision is a lonely act. You alone have to decide, you alone have to act and you alone have to live with the consequences of your decision. No one else can decide for you, nor can anyone else absorb the risks that your decision entails.

Decisions therefore threaten your belief in the existence of an *ultimate rescuer* – someone who by condoning the decision can reassure you, give you strength, share the blame and protect you from criticism; someone who will give you permission, give you their blessing and make it safe.

The fact that, ultimately, we are on our own is not something that can be remedied but something that must be consciously accepted, celebrated and incorporated into our actions.

QUESTION 7

....

Who has the answer?

Rather than understand or accept this, many people prefer instead to constantly run their options past those whose opinion they respect, seeking their advice. Maybe you do, too?

If that's the case, it may surprise you to know that, in truth, no matter from which respected "authority" you choose to get your advice, you've already made up your mind what advice you're going to take by the very act of choosing your adviser.

This is clearly illustrated by a situation in which it's common to take expert advice. When considering what medical treatment you need, you might consider three points of view before deciding whose advice to follow. You may select the consultant who appears pompous but medically seems to know what he or she is talking about, the kind alternative therapist you feel a personal connection with or a friend who says the problem will heal by itself.

By choosing who will be your adviser, you are valuing one kind of *advice* over another. When it comes to the crunch, your next move will depend on whether you believe in medical intervention, value alternative therapies or favour letting your body's recovery take its course.

Even when you choose your adviser as objectively as possible you still decide which bits of the advice to follow, or whether to follow it at all. Once again this decision will be based on *your* values, knowledge and beliefs.

My daughter's having difficulty getting my nine-month-old grandson, Henry, to sleep through the night. Instead of reading books by opinionated amateurs, I want her to read books by child psychologists who use scientific evidence to support their arguments. But then I catch myself thinking, "Yes, but not some autocratic psychologist, whose 'scientific evidence' indicates letting Henry cry himself to sleep." I want her to use the "scientific evidence" cited by *humanistic* psychologists like myself, who advocate liberal views and solutions. As their evidence reflects *my* values, I therefore believe it to be reliable and that this is the correct advice to take!

Ultimately, however much you search around for some authority to advise you, you are left with the inescapable conclusion that by choosing your adviser and then selectively attending to their advice, *you make your own advice*!

Which type of advisers have you chosen, and which parts of their advice are you choosing to ignore and which are you selecting? My hunch is that the advice you're listening to is the advice that fits what you already believe to be true. You have the answer; you just need to listen to yourself, trust yourself and take your own advice.

Self-reflection

To help you embed this point of view, try testing it against your own experience by filling in the columns below:

Chosen adviser	Their advice

For example:

A friend that empathizes with your point of view, not the friend who consistently sees the other side of the argument!

For example:

Leave him within a week.

Advice accepted	Advice rejected	So who makes my advice?
For example:	For example:	For example:
I'm definitely leaving him.	*But I can't possibly manage it in a week!*	*I do!*

THE 64-MILLION-DOLLAR QUESTIONS:

Satisfying your own needs and ambitions

QUESTION 8

....

If not now, when?

Even if you take responsibility for your situation, accept that you make your own advice and make your decision, you may still hesitate to act upon it. You recognize that if you choose to remain in this unacceptable situation you'll have to continue to hide who you really are and what you really want, if you're to keep on fitting in. But, equally, you know that if you choose to be authentic and change, certain people aren't going to like the new you and they're going to be very unpleasant. As the well-known Gestalt psychologist Fritz Perls put it, you have:

> "the choice either to participate in the
> collective psychosis or to take a risk and
> become healthy and perhaps crucified."[1]

If you're chronically dissatisfied with your life, is it because you are participating in the "collective psychosis" of what others expect of you, rather than sticking your neck out and being your own person?

As one client, Jane, expressed it, "The years are going by and I'm feeling it's now or never, but however old the kids get, the demands from them and my husband are as high as they ever were. I don't want to rock the boat, but I'm desperate now to be put first sometimes too, before it's too late."

Do you support everyone in the family at the expense of your own needs, aspirations or ambitions? And do you, in conversations with close friends, ask "When is it my turn?" yet passively continue to obligingly indulge the whims and wishes of everyone else.

Or do you seem to others to be the angry one in control, when in fact you know – and your partner knows – that your partner gets away with murder? Every screaming argument ends with promises that won't be kept, so you're as powerless as those who behave passively; you, too, indulge your partner's lifestyle and ask, "When is it my turn?"

Either way, do you avoid taking a risk and becoming healthy, for fear of perhaps being "crucified"? Or, after each argument, do you naïvely succumb to the "triumph of hope over experience". Your experience tells you that no one else seems to care about your ideas, feelings or ambitions, but you continually hope they will.

Or maybe you say, "I indulge my partner, my children, my friends, parents, grandparents and relatives because I'm a decent human being and I think it's right to do so." That may be true. And yes, on many occasions it's good to put other people first. But given that no one else is about to do it, how about trying to be a decent human being to yourself, too – before it's too late? As Rabbi Hillel wrote in the 10th century BCE:

> "If I am not for myself who will be?
> If I am for myself alone, what am I?
> If not now, when?"

QUESTION 9

....

What's the worst thing that can happen?

It is unlikely that anyone's going to make it easy for you to do something that they either don't agree with or that will make their life harder. Making your change will, therefore, probably result in some pretty uncomfortable conversations, won't it? But if not now, when? Even the most confident of people will avoid disagreeable conversations. Winston Churchill encapsulates this in the following quote about War Cabinet meetings:

> "Why you may take the most gallant sailor, the most intrepid airman or the most audacious solider, put them at a table together – what do you get? The sum of their fears."

When we fail to speak up because it's a potential conflict situation, when we fail to start a discussion about leaving or a conversation about improving the relationship, it's because we fear that we'll either:

- Further damage an already fragile relationship, or
- Hurt the other person or persons, or
- Get hurt by the other person or persons.

So, when clients won't raise the issue of wanting to leave their relationship because they fear how it will affect their parents, I ask, "What's the worst thing that can happen?" And, succumbing to a catastrophic fantasy, they respond, "It'll kill them!"

QUESTION 10

....

Will it really happen?

"Will it really happen?" I enquire. "No," they reply sheepishly.

"Well, what will happen?" "They'll cry. They'll be angry and disappointed in me. They'll worry about not seeing their grandchildren."

And I ask, "And then what will happen, in a year's time when you and the children are settled and in a much happier frame of mind and environment?" To which they reply, grinning, "They'll be happy for me and happy themselves."

So, I suggest raising the issues because:

1. You have no idea if they will or will not be angry or disappointed.

2. They probably feel angry and disappointed with you now!

3. If they feel bad about you for a week or so, so what? You know they'll get over it and feel great about you in due course.

....

QUESTION 11

How does it feel now, standing still?

If you don't tell them it's equally stressful, isn't it? As we have seen, stress and anxiety are an inevitable part of living – whether you go for what you want or deny yourself what you want.

When I explain this to clients, they may still believe their catastrophic fantasies and say, "However bad it is right now, it'll be worse if I try to change things."

I remind them that it's worth considering that life is pretty much 100 percent unpleasant right now. If on the other hand, they take a risk, they have at least a 50/50 chance of it getting better.

Self-reflection

Try answering the following questions:

1. What do I imagine is the worst thing that can happen – what is my catastrophic fantasy?

. . . .

. . . .

. . . .

2. Will it *really* happen?

. . . .

. . . .

. . . .

3. What *will* really happen?

. . . .

. . . .

. . . .

4. What will happen if I don't take the risk?

. . . .

. . . .

. . . .

THE 64-MILLION-DOLLAR QUESTIONS:

Being authentic

....

Who is the real you?

We've seen how every minute of every day you are in situations where you could say one thing and not another; do one thing and not another. But to live an authentic life, you must be aware of your alternatives and also of *the act of considering them*. It's this conscious awareness of your freedom to choose who you are and what you do, at every moment of your life, that defines who can and who cannot claim to be authentic.

On occasion you have a flash of your freedom to be authentic. Driving up the motorway on a sunny afternoon, listening to an uplifting piece of music, for one brief moment of clarity you feel you could do anything with your life and you resolve to make the changes you've thought about for so long – in other words, to follow your own advice. You decide to leave your partner and start your own business; you can make it alone and the kids will survive. Or you decide to stay and make a go of it, telling yourself that it could be a great life if this time you both stick to the agreement to be more appreciative, respectful and accommodating.

But by the time you've parked the car the everyday "reality" that you have created for yourself floods back in and you become swamped once more by the events of your life and absorbed by the values of others. So you return, say, to living the image of spouse and parent, rather than taking the risk of being the person you dreamt of in the car. You return to actualizing *what you think you should be* rather than actualizing *yourself.* As Fritz Perls put it:

> "This difference between *self*-actualizing and self-*image* actualizing is *very* important. Most people only live for their image. Where some people have a self, most people have a void, because they are so busy projecting themselves as this or that."[1]

A self-actualized person is someone who has developed a high level of self-awareness, autonomy and responsibility. Someone who is at one with themselves, free from trying to be someone he or she is not. We self-actualize as we allow ourselves to grow into being who we really are, rather than being cursed with seeking perfection so as to be safe from criticism.

As I said in Chapter 6, because of your fear of disapproval, rejection or looking stupid, you may be in the habit of actualizing your self-image – rather than being self-actualized. Living constantly under the pressure of other people's expectations, you may deny thoughts and feelings that are unacceptable to your partner, parents, friends, religion or society. Eventually, you create a false outer self that covers a denied authentic, inner self. And it is this split into two selves that is so very stressful and helps to make you ill.

QUESTION 13

....

Do you have the courage to be authentic?

To avoid being split, you must fight to live authentically. To be authentic means to be true to yourself, which in turn means being aware of the motives of your actions. Is your behaviour motivated by pride, fear, compassion, pessimism? Or is it rather part of a process of attempting to be real?

Being authentic doesn't mean acting on every impulse. It simply means having integrity in your own eyes by acknowledging and accepting your feelings and thoughts, no matter how unacceptable they may be to others. Only then can you make meaningful choices about how you want to live your life.

So, who is authentic? As the philosopher Van Cleve Morris put it:

> "The individual who is free and who knows
> it. Who knows that every deed and word is
> a choice, and hence an act of value creation
> and who knows that he is author of his own
> life and must be held personally responsible
> ... and that these values cannot be justified
> by conforming to something or somebody
> outside himself."[2]

QUESTION 14

....

Are you succumbing to the Gulliver Effect?

Rather than be true to your own values, and so risk being different, disagreeing, confronting or acting autonomously, it may be that you justify your choices "by conforming to something or somebody outside" yourself – to your friends, parents, partner, community or society.

How authentic are you? Are you choosing your own values and living by them or are you being what you think others want you to be? If you don't courageously speak out for what you believe in and make your dreams a reality, you become a bland version of yourself. Indeed, maybe you're worried that you've already changed so much that you no longer recognize yourself.

This change for the worse is what I call the Gulliver Effect. During his seafaring expeditions, Jonathan Swift's Gulliver is shipwrecked on an island called Lilliput. He awakes to find himself tied down by the island's tiny inhabitants. Gulliver, being a giant to the Lilliputians, could easily have freed himself from their threads, but felt unable to do so for fear of crushing the Lilliputians, being hurt himself by their miniature arrows or simply making matters worse.

Feeling shackled by invisible threads, we suffer the Gulliver Effect when day after day we accommodate others. We tolerate what we know to be wrong because we make false assumptions about our rights, the rights of others and the probable outcome of standing up for what we believe in.

QUESTION 15

....

Have you shackled yourself with invisible threads?

Do you suffer from the Gulliver Effect? Do you feel shackled by invisible threads, silently disagreeing with your partner's behaviour, values or attitudes, only to voice your real thoughts when you feel safe with those you can trust?

Or do you put up with an unsatisfactory situation for too long until you finally explode, freeing yourself from the invisible threads but stressing yourself, hurting others and making matters worse in the process? When we do finally cry, "Enough!", just as Gulliver eventually did, we do so in a way that is both self-destructive and destructive to others. Paradoxically, we do precisely what we've been trying to avoid.

Maria is a wife and mother of three. Though once a partici-pating, engaged mum, Maria has become a morose figure who is saying less and less. Why? Because close family members have exploited her accommodating nature in order to advance their own paths. She has given in to her demanding children and husband, yet has met with no reciprocal behaviour when she tries to suggest that she spends time becoming an interior designer.

So the change for the worse has occurred. She began as a generous, loving wife and mother, giving of her all. Everyone stood to get the best of her. When she began to want her own time, space and career, but was faced with objections from every member of the family, she accommodated and silently went about her duties while loudly complaining to friends and other relatives behind her family's backs. Every now and again, Maria's frustration spills over when she verbally attacks her children or husband.

The home is Maria's Lilliput. Trying for years to accommodate her family she felt like a square peg in a round hole, and is now bent out of shape. Her talents are lost to her. She is demotivated, distant and unhappy.

Because finding satisfying values and living by them is a lonely and highly individual matter, you may see your freedom to be authentic as a curse that you try to avoid. But you could equally view it as a challenge to make something worthwhile of your life.

If you want to rise to your challenge, you will need to summon the courage to break away from your old patterns, to stand alone and find your own meaning. You will need to face your fears, challenge your negative language and overcome your pride, excessive compassion or pessimism. You will then be free to make your decision once and for all and take responsibility for the life you choose to live.

Self-reflection

Try answering the following questions:

1. How do I *actualize my self-image* in my daily activities?

. . . .

. . . .

. . . .

. . . .

. . . .

. . . .

2. If I were *self-actualizing*, what would I be doing differently?

. . . .

. . . .

. . . .

. . . .

. . . .

. . . .

CHAPTER 10

LET'S TAKE A BREATHER

This is a good place to recap the previous four chapters. The 64-Million-Dollar Questions posed in those chapters outline the philosophy I'd like you to hold in your head to liberate you from your indecision:

- Who are you trying to please?
- Are you your own jailor?
- Who's pulling your strings?
- What are you waiting for?
- Are you avoiding responsibility for the years already wasted?
- Are you hoping someone will hold your hand?
- Who has the answer?
- If not now, when?
- What's the worst thing that can happen?
- Will it really happen?

- How does it feel now, standing still?
- Who is the real you?
- Do you have the courage to be authentic?
- Are you succumbing to the Gulliver Effect?
- Have you shackled yourself with invisible threads?

The Six Life-Changing Hurdles

To help make this philosophy user-friendly, I've distilled it into Six Life-Changing Hurdles. If you're to ensure that you have a fulfilled life, rather than a wasted one, from this day on you must overcome these Six Life-Changing Hurdles:

1. Be authentic – take the risk of being yourself
   (*not what everyone else wants you to be*)

2. Accept anxiety as a positive, fundamental human experience (*stop giving in to it*)

3. Make your one and only life a meaningful one
   (*not one that you'll end up regretting*)

4. Take responsibility for your situation
   (*no blaming others*)

5. Be aware that you always have a choice
   (*you're not as trapped as you think you are*)

6. Live by your own values and standards
   (*not everyone else's*)

Armed with this newfound perspective on your life, you should now be clear which decision to take – stay or leave. And this philosophy should also provide you with the courage to do it now. So:

I've told you what you're doing.

I've told you why you're doing it.

And I've told you what you have to do:

Jump the Six Life-Changing Hurdles!

You have enough to do it now – this could be the end of the book.

Just jump!

But my hunch is you're now saying, "Yes, but *how* do I do it?"

Despite learning my philosophy, many of my clients still find themselves too frightened to jump into the abyss. I repeat to them, and repeat to you: no one can jump for you. You alone have to decide, and live with the consequences. No one can make it easy for you. When all is said and done, you are alone in suffering the guilt of remaining unfulfilled and you will be alone in suffering the anxiety of taking a risk by crossing your Rubicon.

So the answer to your dilemma must surely be, "Just jump!" It's either that or stay the same. If you want to live a more valuable life – one in which you continuously change, develop and fulfil your potential by acting, evaluating and acting again – you'll need to jump the six hurdles every single day.

The phrase "life is a journey" has been well and truly reiterated but the pain of travelling alone has not. It's lonely, it's painful, it's tough and it's all there is! There isn't anything else.

There is no given, no ultimate guru, no Buddha, no right answer, no authority, just you. I have indicated the way forward and you can find someone's hand to hold to give you confidence. But it's like bungee jumping. Someone can show you how to strap yourself into the harness, describe how it will feel, explain the best technique to avoid damaging yourself and even hold your hand before you go, but in the final moment you and you alone must jump. Once you have made your decision, you will have to go through any pain alone.

I do realize, however, that even though the philosophy gives you the courage to act now, this is only half the battle. You're standing on the edge of the abyss. Now you need to learn how to jump skilfully.

So I'm going to reiterate in Part III what I've said in Parts I and II, but in a more pragmatic way. I will give you some techniques to help you implement your decision sensitively. But remember that, in the end, it still comes down to the fact that you'll have to jump alone …

PART III

THE SIX LIFE-CHANGING HURDLES

CHAPTER 11

HURDLE

1

Be authentic – take the risk of being yourself

(not what everyone else wants you to be)

Be authentic

Your first hurdle is to take the risk of being yourself and living authentically. To do this you need to ask yourself, "Will I commit myself to a course of action and engage in life as my own person? Or will I remain inauthentic and merely continue as I am now – occupying roles and going through the motions without real commitment?"

Our inauthenticity is most obvious when we want to say what we think, be who we are or do what we want, but stop ourselves because we know that the people around us won't like it. Instead we prefer to avoid the inevitable conflict.

Let's take the examples of Christmas with the family, being interviewed for a new job and going on a first date with someone you really like. On each of these occasions, it's likely that to some extent you're not being your real self because you are censoring yourself – holding back things you think others might not like. This is you being inauthentic.

Of course, in some situations, such as the ones I've just described, it's a good idea to conform to what other people want and expect of you. You want everyone to get along at Christmas, to make a good impression during your interview and to be asked on a second date!

But it's unhealthy to behave like this all the time. Habitually behaving inauthentically to please others *against your will* eventually impacts on your self-respect, happiness and even your very existence.

So your first hurdle is to learn how to be authentic – to be yourself and say what you really think even when you anticipate that the people around you don't want to hear it.

When you are authentic, you stick to the courage of your convictions and don't compromise over what's really important to you, even if that makes you feel uncomfortable. You deal with improving the relationship if you've decided to stay; deal with the arguments if you've decided to go; overcome all the objections and concerns of family and friends; manage officious solicitors, snooty estate agents and other professionals.

Know how you argue

Conflict in itself is not the problem. It's how we handle it. You may find this surprising because when you think of the word conflict you associate it with anger, shouting, slammed doors, war, win–lose, sarcasm, hurt, upset, sulking, crying, name-calling, insults and general unpleasantness. So, surely, conflict *is* the problem.

But think of some positive words that you associate with conflict and the benefits that conflict can ultimately bring. What about creativity, discussion, clarity, problem-solving, communication, optimism, empathy, agreement, solutions, win–win, peace, understanding, improvement and change?

Conflict in itself is neither negative nor positive. It is neutral. What makes it either constructive or destructive is the way we manage it.

A great way to understand your inauthentic and authentic behaviour is to consider how you handle conflict. Ask yourself the following:

1. Cooperativeness: During an argument, how much do I really try to understand my partner's point of view? Do I *cooperatively* question and listen, or *uncooperatively* override it?

2. Assertiveness: During an argument, how much do I *assert* my honest opinion? Do I courageously express what I think or feel or do I tend not to speak my mind?

Then, keeping these two ways of behaving in mind, look at Model 2 on page 90 and select the box that most typifies the way you manage conflict: – Competing, Collaborating, Compromising, Avoiding or Accommodating.

Don't succumb to the Gulliver Effect

When they do this exercise, most of my clients recognize that in life generally, and during conflict specifically, they tend to avoid, accommodate or compromise. In other words, they sit in the bottom triangle of the model.

This is because, during disagreements, their partner tends to forcefully compete (top-left box in the Gulliver Effect

Model 2: The Gulliver Effect[1]

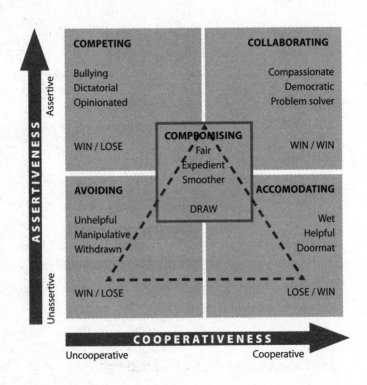

model) and this makes them nervous, uneasy and reluctant to argue back.

Or their partner says nothing, supposedly avoiding conflict, while their face makes their contempt clear (bottom-left box). This passive-aggressive mode of handling conflict can be equally intimidating, leaving the other person reluctant to start an argument they rarely win.

The triangle at the bottom of the model is a visual image of the Gulliver Effect. Do you recognize these patterns of handling conflicts? Are you intimidated by your partner's style of handling conflict and, consequently, feeling "shackled by invisible threads", do you opt to stay in the Gulliver Effect triangle, accommodating, avoiding or compromising?

Do you do that with the family at Christmas, with your boss or team at work, with friends, with shoddy workmen, during a bad haircut or in response to offhand service in a restaurant?

Stop thinking "anything for peace"

If you recognize yourself as someone who lives in the bottom triangle, especially in the Accommodating box, then you probably rationalize your behaviour by telling yourself and others "anything for peace". You're right – by avoiding disagreements, unpleasantness, anger and arguments, in the short term it's peaceful.

But what about the long term? If you live your life like that, day after day, night after night, month after month and year after year, accommodating an unacceptable situation in order to avoid an unpleasant scene or make matters worse, it's anything but peaceful, isn't it? Eventually, you feel like a doormat. You consistently give into other people's bad attitude and behaviour, prioritize their wants at the expense of your own, and eventually ask yourself, "When is it my turn?"

A lifeless routine with no passion, simply saying "Yes" to others is an insult to your integrity. To give up your integrity for the sake of a few minutes', days' or weeks' peace is a huge price to pay.

Now is the time to change your behaviour. Catch yourself thinking "anything for peace" and remind yourself that, in the long term, putting up with what is unacceptable to you is anything but peaceful. Looking back with regret at how people took advantage of your good nature will, I guarantee, be stressful – if it isn't already.

Stop "losing it"

On the other hand, you may recognize yourself as someone who handles conflict from the top-left box of the Gulliver Effect model, constantly shouting at your partner during arguments while *they* sit in the bottom triangle.

Whether you're angrily competing or sitting in the bottom triangle accommodating, avoiding or compromising, you're being equally inauthentic. If you or your partner remain silent during conflict, the lack of authenticity is pretty obvious. But it may surprise you to learn that, even when one of you is angrily attacking the other, you're still most likely not being authentic.

I was recently in an office with a colleague of mine, Nigel, who was looking worried. In reply to my asking why, he said he'd just upset his girlfriend, Emma. Nigel said not only did he feel sorry that he'd upset her, but also that he was apprehensive about speaking to her again because Emma had a pretty bad temper. I knew this to be true.

Yet when Emma next phoned, Nigel snapped his one-word replies and sarcastic comments and finally put down the receiver without a goodbye. Nigel's angry words hid his feelings of hurt, guilt and apprehension. Because of his inauthentic behaviour, Emma had completely the wrong impression of his true state of mind. My hunch is that the hostility between them escalated at home that evening.

Had Nigel been authentic and calmly explained why he'd done what he'd done and how he felt about Emma's attack, he and Emma would have had a far greater chance of resolving their differences.

If you're anything like Nigel, you keep "losing it" and screaming with frustration in the hope that one day you will get your point across and change your partner's behaviour.

You never do and now it's likely that not only do you dislike your partner's behaviour, but you're also appalled at your own. Your rage hides your feelings of hurt, frustration and apprehension. As time goes on, you both go over and over the same ground yet nothing changes. You are at a loss as to what else you can do to get what you want from the relationship and feel increasingly angry at your partner's intransigence; an intransigence that completely disempowers you.

Get the truth on the table

No matter who in the relationship is behaving aggressively or passive-aggressively (hiding feelings of insecurity, jealousy and so on), you can guarantee that the other person will avoid, accommodate or compromise. Equally, if one or two people intimidate during a Christmas family gathering or a dinner party, then the others will sit "shackled by invisible threads" and accommodate, avoid or compromise; their ideas and opinions will remain unvoiced or watered down.

So the truth is never on the table. And if the truth is never on the table, you never discuss or resolve the real problems. As the African-American writer James Baldwin puts it:

> "Not everything that is faced can be changed,
> but nothing can be changed until it is faced."

Carey and Robert had the following pattern of handling disagreements. Initially, Carey would collaboratively explain to Robert what she wanted. On one occasion she wanted him to paint the front room blue. Robert hates painting and the colour blue, but as he has an "anything for peace" approach, to avoid an argument he said, "Great idea."

Three weeks later, Robert's done nothing. Carey, feeling

angry, was now in the competing mode, and aggressively asked, "Why haven't you painted the front room yet?" Robert put up a little resistance, but then thought "anything for peace" and accommodatingly "agreed" to paint the room blue in the coming weeks, while having no intention of doing so.

Three weeks later, Carey is now shouting at Robert about his lack of effort and that "typically", once again, he doesn't keep his promises! To avoid conflict Robert now not only psychologically removes himself from an argument by giving in, but physically removes himself, too. He spends his free time in the shed at the bottom of the garden or in the pub complaining with male friends about nagging wives.

So whose fault is it that Robert's truth is never on the table? Carey's, because the threat of her anger means that Robert is scared to speak up? Or Robert's, because he lacks the courage to say what he really thinks and feels?

Unshackle yourself

Well, we now know that no one can blame anyone else for his or her own behaviour. Had Robert had the courage right at the start to say in an adult–adult, collaborative, problem-solving tone, "I don't want to do the painting and I hate blue", Carey could then have responded by rationally discussing options, such as hiring a decorator and choosing a colour they both liked.

By believing it was OK to be himself, not what Carey wanted him to be, Robert would have put them both in the win–win, problem-solving Collaborating box top-right of the model – the matter resolved, stress avoided, the subject closed. Robert could have chosen to have the courage of his convictions and speak out – he's not as trapped as he and his mates in the pub think they are.

If you're to have an authentic relationship you have to decide what differences you need to address and what truths you need to get on the table, and then handle conflict collaboratively.

Stop succumbing to an unspoken contract

If you consistently fail to resolve the differences with your partner then you are not just wasting your time – you are wasting your life. It is a tragedy that you neither give up and leave nor *skilfully* resolve your differences and stay. Instead, you stay and endlessly argue or silently seethe, while continually threatening to, or thinking about, splitting up. You end up living together with an unspoken, implicit contract – an expectation that you:

- Don't say what you mean
- Don't do what you say
- Don't respect each other
- Don't listen to each other
- Raise opinions and issues with a counsellor, friends or family rather than with your partner
- Don't show spontaneous affection
- Blame each other for your own feelings and behaviour

- Don't make time for each other
- Take silence as agreement
- Play games and manipulate
- Don't trust each other
- Resist change
- Make shallow agreements
- Don't stick to commitments.

Whether you stay or go, if you're to live the life you want to lead, you're going to have to do things differently. So you'll need an *explicit* contract whereby you agree to allow each other to be authentic. (In the Appendix, I've described how you could change your implicit contract to an explicit one.)

You need to experiment with new behaviour and be who you want to be, telling each other what's on your minds in a calm and rational way; saying what you mean, listening to each other, raising opinions and issues as and when they arise and not with friends after the event, making real decisions and sticking to commitments.

Be authentic but ethical

If you stay you'll want to work together at getting the best out of the relationship. You need to develop an authentic relationship, in which you both feel free to be yourselves, combining your strengths while compensating for your weaknesses. And if you want a real chance of making it work, you need to combine being authentic with being ethical. This means exhibiting in your behaviour the following four principles:

1. Be respectful: don't treat your partner as a means to your ends. For example, don't allow your partner to keep the place clean while professing indifference to cleanliness, so avoiding lifting a finger when in reality cleanliness does matter to you.

2. Be considerate: don't be self-centred. Refrain from advancing your own ambitions at the expense of others. You have a responsibility to listen to your partner and make decisions that are beneficial and not harmful to him or her. For example, don't stay out drinking with friends night after night leaving your partner bored and alone, or frazzled at your children's bath and bedtime.

3. Be fair: no one should get special treatment, except when the situation demands it. Reasons for unequal treatment must be clear and reasonable; for example, if a woman is heavily pregnant or when the man's job provides a lifestyle that everyone appreciates yet demands long hours away from home.

4. Be honest: dishonesty may well result in unpleasant consequences. It puts a strain on how you as a couple connect with each other. Your impact is compromised because your partner no longer believes in you.

Complete truth can be destructive, however – the answer to "Does my bum look big in this" may be a dishonest, yet caring "No", if there's no time to change! Yet, later, you may want to convey the opposite using consideration and respect to avoid offence. A tactful person can tell you something you don't want to hear and you'll be thankful for the information. So the challenge is to strike a balance: it's important to be authentic, but also essential to be sensitive to the feelings of your partner.

Being authentic and ethical means not promising what you can't deliver, not misrepresenting, not hiding behind evasions, not evading accountability and not believing that your needs release you from the responsibility to respect your partner's dignity and humanity.

If, by being honest and ethical, your relationship rebalances itself in a way that makes you feel optimistic and happy, and your partner feels that way too, then that's great.

If, on the other hand, your being authentic and ethical makes your incompatibility even more obvious, then it's time to leave decently, knowing that you have tried everything. You've tried being the person your partner wants, and tried being the real you, but neither makes the two of you happy.

HURDLE

2

Accept anxiety as a positive, fundamental human experience

(stop giving in to it)

See anxiety as life energy

Whenever we are in any position on the conflict model other than the top-right, Collaborating box – that is, whenever we compete, accommodate, avoid or compromise – it's because we see our situation, the other person or our options as a threat.

Starting an argument, lowering our standard of living or announcing our separation to others can all be viewed as a threat to our self-image, our ego or our comfort zone. And when we see something as a threat, our anxiety levels automatically rise and we tend to behave either unskilfully or indecisively.

So your second hurdle is to learn to accept this anxiety as a positive, fundamental human experience, an inevitable part of being free. Rather than give into it, you need to view anxiety as a sign that you are either going to be unskilful or indecisive. Check your anxiety and then use it constructively, seeing it not as a symptom of looming catastrophe but as life energy. As Kierkegaard put it:

> "It's an adventure that every person must undertake – to learn how to be anxious in order that he may not perish, either by never having experienced anxiety or by succumbing to it. Anyone who has learned to be anxious in the right way has learned the ultimate."[1]

I am going to show you my Facing Challenges Technique, which will help you to anticipate and use life's inevitable anxiety "in order that you may not perish" and to learn "to be anxious in the right way".

You may be thinking, "Beverley has said that I have no choice but to suffer anxiety (stress) if I cross my Rubicon, or guilt (stress) if I don't. So, I *can't* choose how I feel."

But I'm going to show how you *can* choose how you feel and how you handle your feelings.

Think "problem" not "threat"

When we perceive a threat, our autonomic nervous system pumps adrenalin into the bloodstream. We experience shallow breathing, a red face, increased heart rate, perspiration, dry mouth, muscle tension and so on – the physical signs of anxiety and stress. People recognize experiencing symptoms like these when they're about to speak in public, or walk into a job interview or face a group of strangers in a social setting.

This automatic reaction to a "threat" mobilizes the body for "fight or flight". Put simply, shallow breathing oxygenates the blood, which the heart pumps faster to muscles that are tense in anticipation of fighting the threat or running from it.

As a reaction this worked when we were cavemen and women confronting a large animal and had to choose to either kill it for lunch or run for our lives. But nowadays, all too often we see things as threats that are really just problems to be solved.

- Is telling your parents you don't want to come to Christmas this year a threat or a problem to be solved?
- Is downsizing to a smaller house a threat or a problem to be solved?
- Is walking your children into a new school a threat or a problem to be solved?
- Is dividing your possessions a threat or a problem to be solved?
- Is challenging your partner's habits and attitude a threat or a problem to be solved?

The problem with succumbing to the flight response (withdrawing, giving up, giving in, smoothing over, agreeing, avoiding, accommodating, removing yourself) or the fight response (forcefully making statements, over-talking, slamming doors, shouting, being sarcastic, hitting out, throwing things) is that you never solve the problem, do you?

Say you walk into the house and your partner, with his or her back to you, grunts an aggressive "hello". You may feel threatened by the likelihood of an unpleasant argument and, instead of asking what's wrong, you walk into the living room, pick up the newspaper and hope the atmosphere blows over. But does it? No. The flight response either makes the problem worse or postpones it, but never solves it.

Similarly, if your partner's rudeness makes your heart rate increase and you respond to the tone of voice by starting a raging argument, you won't solve the underlying problem either because – fight or flight – the truth is never on the table.

Choose your viewpoint

The first step to using anxiety in the right way is to take responsibility for your heart rate going up, along with all the other bodily changes that accompany your fight-or-flight response. And stop blaming your partner or your situation. You have to recognize that it's not your partner or the situation itself that stresses you – or makes you feel anything, for that matter.

We tend to assume that being stuck in heavy traffic on a motorway makes us feel angry and drive carelessly, or that listening to music makes us feel sad and cry, or that it's our partner's laziness that makes us feel frustrated and causes us to nag. We imagine that the situation causes our feelings and that we then behave accordingly:

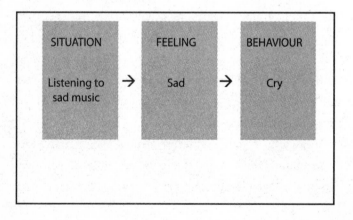

Let's use the example of your crossing the Rubicon of leaving your relationship. You may say that the uncertainty associated with leaving makes you anxious and that this causes you to vacillate indecisively. But does everyone who contemplates crossing their Rubicon of leaving a relationship feel anxious and hence vacillate? The answer must surely be no, because people do leave relationships.

Some people are excited by the prospect of change and going it alone. Others are relieved at the thought of leaving an unacceptable situation and having the opportunity to start again. Some feel happy at the thought of leaving because they're sure it will be better for everyone involved.

In the following example, four people are responding to the same situation with four different feelings and behaviours, so it is clear that it is not the *situation* that is causing the feelings and behaviour:

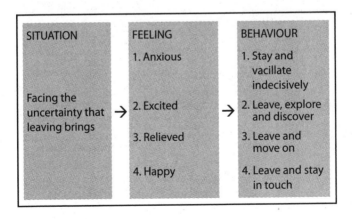

What causes our feelings is the way we *think* about the situation – how we decide to *view* it, our *interpretation* and our *expectations*. As the psychiatrist Victor Frankl, reflecting on his internment in a Nazi concentration camp, put it:

> "In the living laboratories of the concentration
> camp, we watched comrades behaving like
> swine whilst others behaved like saints; man
> has both potentialities within himself. Which
> one he actualizes depends on decisions, not
> on conditions."[2]

It's how you decide to think about your condition that causes your feelings and subsequent behaviour, not the condition itself.

SITUATION		THOUGHTS	
		1. Who knows what's on the other side? I'm scared that I'm making a big mistake.	
Crossing your Rubicon: leaving and facing the uncertainty that this brings	→	2. Wow, I'm free! I can do anything with my life.	→
		3. Finally I'm out – anything has got to be better than this.	
		4. This is the best thing for everyone and we're going to make it work.	

If you are to control your anxiety you need to change the way you view things. You have to stop viewing problems as threats.

Choose your feelings

To illustrate this further, the diagram shown below gives four ways in which you could decide to think about crossing your Rubicon. Each way of thinking might cause one of four different feelings that in turn might result in one of the four potential behaviours described.

What are you saying to yourself to make yourself feel anxious? Try thinking the opposite and see the effect it has on how you feel.

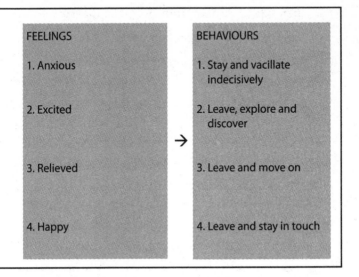

FEELINGS	BEHAVIOURS
1. Anxious	1. Stay and vacillate indecisively
2. Excited	2. Leave, explore and discover
3. Relieved	3. Leave and move on
4. Happy	4. Leave and stay in touch

Change the situation or the way you view it

You need to decide either to change your situation or to change the way you view it. There is no point remaining in the same situation and continuing to view it with stress, horror or unhappiness. That's just a waste of energy.

You could choose to remain in the same situation but view it differently – and still be authentic. Being authentic doesn't necessarily involve changing your circumstances:

> "Before he is enlightened, a man gets up each
> morning to spend the day tending his fields,
> returns home to eat his supper, goes to bed,
> makes love to his woman and falls asleep. But
> once he has attained enlightenment, then a
> man gets up each morning to spend the day
> tending his fields, returns home to eat his
> supper, goes to bed, makes love to his woman
> and falls asleep."[3]

Stephanie had a generally good and loving relationship with her partner, Simon. But she constantly thought of leaving because she found Simon's selfishness in spending nights out in clubs without her thoughtless and upsetting.

Stephanie's inability to change Simon's behaviour, no matter what she did, made her feel that she had no choice but to stay trapped in an unhappy relationship, unable to leave because of their shared obligations. However, once she realized that her jail was of her own making and that she was in fact free to choose to stay or leave him at any time, it became clear to her that she loved Simon. The sense of freedom enabled Stephanie to choose to remain in an apparently unchangeable relationship but, instead, change her mindset; to relax into the situation, accept Simon for who he was and relish those aspects of his personality that she loved.

If you know that you are free to leave your relationship or change it, yet consciously choose to stay with no attempt at change, you will no longer experience tension. Like the man tending the field before and after enlightenment, though outwardly your life looks the same, your mindset has changed. Because you now see that you are free to move on but choose not to, you take responsibility for making the most of your partnership as it is.

No one can make you feel anything

So, when you contemplate crossing your Rubicon, you can decide to think about it in a variety of ways. How you think will shape your feelings, and your subsequent behaviour will reflect those feelings.

To take responsibility for your fear and indecisiveness, and to learn to be anxious in the right way, you must first accept that your feelings are caused by things that go on *inside* your head rather than by the things that go on *outside*. As the Stoic philosopher Epictetus said in 100 CE:

> "Men are not disturbed by things but by the
> views they take of them."

No one can make you feel anything. Whatever anyone else says, thinks or does, your feelings result from the way you interpret it. If a friend implies your decision is immoral, you can laugh because you think she's stupid, cry because you value her opinion of you or shrug indifferently because her opinion means nothing to you. Alternatively, you can simply think it's an interesting point of view. This will help you remain logical and calm and in a better position to resolve collaboratively the problem between you.

In the 1995 film *Get Shorty*, John Travolta makes a relevant point when his co-star Rene Russo asks after a fight, "Were you scared?" And he replies, "Yes." To which she responds, "You don't look scared" and he says, "I'm not now, I was then. How long do you want me to feel scared?" He is aware that he can choose what he feels and how long he feels it, because his feelings merely reflect his thinking.

The Facing Challenges Technique

Don't respond to situations, disagreements, conflict or difficult people with anxiety, blame, anger or depression. Instead, meet life challenges with courage and compassion by following this four-step technique. For example, if someone is challenging your point of view:

1. **Recognize physiological changes as a sign** Use the changes caused by adrenalin as signs that you're going into unskilful flight or fight. (I feel a throb in my throat; you may get a knot in your stomach, reddening of your neck, sweaty hands and so on.) Think the word "RELAX" and relax tense shoulder and neck muscles. Then change your negative self-talk. Say to yourself, "It's just an interesting point of view" four times (which will take about eight seconds) while the other person is still talking. This will enable you to:

2. **Change the way you view your provoker** Tell yourself that he or she is fine as a person, you just don't like what they're saying, or how they're saying it or their behaviour. Remember that many people are not feeling OK about themselves no matter how they behave, so tune into that and be compassionate.

3. **Change the way you view the provocation** Tell yourself, "It's not personal. It's just an interesting point of view. My heart rate doesn't have to go up one jot. He might be 100 percent right or I might be. Let's start at 50/50. Let's discuss it and see."

4. **Problem-solve by asking a question** If you make a statement you'll sound defensive, as you'll either belittle yourself and your ideas or the other person

and his or her ideas. It's fight or flight again. Instead, use the words, "That's interesting, what makes you say that?" They feel empathic as it sounds as if you're trying to find out about, and cooperate with, the other person's point of view. It also gives you more time to calm down while the other person is answering.

And remember, this is not a subtle way of manipulating people – you don't have to win!

You need to practise these skills, just as you did when you learnt to drive or play golf. But as you practise them, you'll find you begin to follow the Facing Challenges Technique on autopilot, just as you do when you drive.

If you accept anxiety as something that will always accompany crossing a Rubicon, you can learn to control your feelings by viewing challenging people and situations differently. You'll soon find yourself being anxious in the right way and skilfully crossing your Rubicons.

The difference between risk-taking entrepreneurs and others is that, like Imad in Chapter 3, the former view crossing their Rubicons and making mistakes as learning experiences that make them more authentic individuals – and better partners, too. And so can you.

Self-reflection

Here are some sentences to complete with one or two words that accurately describe your feelings. Focus on how you feel about the other person or situation described:

1. When someone is overdependent on me I feel ....

....

....

2. When someone gets angry with me I feel ....

....

3. When some puts me down I feel ....

....

4. When I imagine leaving I feel ....

....

5. When I imagine staying I feel ....

....

Now try filling in the opposite feelings for each statement. What needs to change for you to feel differently about the same situation? So, once again, what or *who* makes you feel powerless, stressed, trapped, belittled or anxious …?!

CHAPTER 13

HURDLE

3

Make your one and only life a meaningful one

(not one you'll end up regretting)

Stop behaving like a tangled monkey

Some clients say, "It's all very well telling me that I need to change my negative self-talk to positive, but I can't control my thoughts. I'm so overwhelmed by them that I wake up sweating in the night. My mind goes over and over options and problems, even when I'm asleep. And I obsessively churn over ideas during the day. Sometimes I'm so deep in thought driving down the motorway that I miss my exit!"

The Buddhist monk and author Matthieu Ricard compares our inability to calm our turbulent mind to a monkey tethered by a number of ropes. The more the monkey struggles to be free, the more tangled he becomes. Eventually, he is so tied up in knots that neither he nor anyone else can help him to straighten out the ropes.[1]

Maybe you empathize with the monkey, your thoughts becoming more entangled the more you struggle for clarity. What you need is a technique to calm your muddled thoughts and put things into perspective. Only then will you be able to take a rational decision, one that will ensure you jump your third hurdle to make your one and only life a meaningful one, not one you'll end up regretting.

If you're to eliminate obsessive, anxious self-talk, you need to learn how to "stay in the here and now". You've probably heard that phrase before, but what does "stay in the here and now" really mean? Many of us will be familiar with the following scenario that illustrates the point:

Imagine your partner was being difficult and demeaning at a barbeque with friends. He or she could not or would not see your point of view. You drive home grinding your teeth, beeping your horn, frustrated and angry, thinking to yourself, "He shouldn't have spoken to me like that" or "I should have answered her more strongly." You arrive home having gone through four sets of traffic lights and don't remember any of them.

Later, you sit down to eat dinner together in silence. You eat very fast because all the time you are thinking, "How could he speak to me like that?" or "Why did I let her get away with it?" and "How can I face my friends next time we see them?" You have indigestion. You sit in front of the television but you don't see much because all the time the argument is swimming in front of your eyes and the same thoughts are going through your head. Now you have a cracking headache.

Finally you go to bed. As your partner wants to read you pick up a book, but you read the same paragraph four times and still can't remember what it says. So you put your book down. Your partner falls asleep and finally you drop off. In the middle of the night, you wake with a start, your heart is going like the clappers and off you go again: "Why didn't I answer back in the same tone?", "I don't need to put up with this", "I'm dreading the atmosphere in the morning – not again."

Stop living in the past and future

What is it that's making you anxious? Is there anything in the bedroom that's aggravating you at that moment? Is it the duvet, your soundly sleeping partner, the ceiling? No. There is nothing that is actually happening in the *here and now* that's stressful. It's only your thoughts that are making you anxious. And these thoughts are about the argument yesterday and about how you're going to handle yourself tomorrow. So, my definition of anxiety and how to overcome it is as follows:

> Anxiety is rehearsing for tomorrow
> and reliving the past.
> Stay in the here and now.

You need a technique that helps you to stay in the here and now and either do something constructive at 3 o'clock in the morning, like write a "to do" list, or go back to sleep. Otherwise, your self-talk simply exhausts you and wastes energy that could be used to solve the problem the following day. If you're to face your anxiety and use it constructively you have to learn to control your thoughts.

Stop living in a fantasy world

The problem, as we've seen, is that you're probably very talented at living in a fantasy world of self-talk. You've spent weeks, months, even years, aggravating yourself over things that happened in the past and your fears about your plans for the future. Otherwise, chances are you wouldn't be reading this book! And as you know, living in the past and future is a never-ending downward spiral.

Liz complained that when she was at work, she constantly worried about her marriage and its impact on her children, and that when she was with her children at home she constantly worried about work. Neither work nor her marriage and children benefited from her presence. By learning to stay in the here and now using the technique I describe below, she could spend 100 percent of her energy on her children and marriage when at home and 100 percent of her energy on work when she was at the office. Everyone benefited.

Staying in the here and now will help you to catch your negative self-talk, change it to something more constructive and feel more positive, optimistic and courageous. You'll be more open, honest and decisive and this will encourage you to take positive action.

To stay in the here and now, it is helpful to consider experience as consisting of three areas of awareness:

1. **Internal reality** is anything experienced inside the body right now. You might say, "I can feel that my mouth is dry, I can feel my elbow is resting on the table and my right knee has a slight pain in it." No one can dispute that this is how you experience yourself right now.

2. **External reality** consists of awareness of the external world right here and right now. You might say, "I can see

a bunch of red roses and there is a bright light shining from the ceiling. I can see trees outside the window; they are moving." External reality relates to what you experience, without interpretation. If you were to say, "The trees are moving in the wind", it would be fantasy (the third area of awareness). Perhaps the trees are moving because the little boy next door is climbing in them or your neighbours are shaking down apples!

3. **Fantasy** consists of interpretations, assumptions or opinions. You might say, "I can see my partner at the computer. She has a frown on her face." If you add, "She's looking worried", that's a fantasy. She may simply be concentrating. Fantasies, then, are assumptions about, and interpretations of, the world around us. They are thoughts that are outside internal and external reality.

Fantasy is an important part of life. It is the basis of creativity, of art and literature. Fantasizing can be relaxing, as when you are reminiscing happily about your relationship or perfect holiday. We also use fantasies to make plans: whether to remain workaholics in order to buy a big house, or stay in the flat and have more money and time for leisure; and whether to stay or go.

Fantasy can also be destructive. Because fantasies are often catastrophic – visualizations of the worst possible scenario – we tend to respond with either "fight" or "flight". For example, your partner forgets your anniversary. You immediately interpret this as proof that they think less of you than they used to. You spend a dreadful day fantasizing about this, feeling more and more upset and angry or withdrawn, only to find out that they've arranged a surprise meal at your favourite restaurant followed by the concert that you've been longing to see.

What distinguishes fruitful fantasy from destructive fantasy is that people take strength or act on the former, while merely aggravating themselves with the latter. Fantasy is a waste of energy if you don't act on it. You book the holiday. You remain in the smaller house and enjoy a more rounded lifestyle. You paint the picture or write the book. You give yourself space to reminisce and relax. You stay or you leave.

Stay in the here and now

Staying in the here and now means consciously blocking out destructive fantasies by remaining in internal and external reality.

Anne recounted how she successfully used this technique while queuing to buy a train ticket on her way to collect her children from school. Ten people were in front of her. After five minutes of standing on the same spot, she began to think that the man at the window was writing his memoirs, not just a cheque to pay for his ticket. Worrying (fantasizing) about what would happen to the children and her reputation with the teachers if she were late, her heart rate began to increase. She began to perspire. She imagined herself grabbing the man by the scruff of his neck and dragging him away from the window, screaming at him to stand aside while she bought her ticket.

Catching herself aggravating herself, she asked if she really intended to do what she had imagined. Was she going to act out her fantasy? The answer, not surprisingly, was "No".

At this point, she said to herself, "Okay, if I'm not going to do anything, relax. Get into the here and now. Stop fantasizing about what my girls will feel if I'm late and what the teachers will say. The critical remarks will come whether I worry or not. So the best thing for me to do is conserve my energy and not worry."

She focused on internal and external reality. "There is a newspaper stand next to me and I can see *The Times*. I can see a woman in front of me wearing a red hat. I can feel myself take a deep breath and I am aware of the tension across my eyes. It is easing a little."

Rather than fantasizing about the past or future, she used her energy to make a rational decision regarding the choices she had in her current situation.

To finish Anne's story: she bought her ticket, caught the train and wasn't late to pick up the children. She arrived relaxed with plenty of energy to use where it was appropriate – in happily greeting her girls and whisking them off for an ice-cream. And even if she'd arrived late, she could still have arrived either late and frazzled or late and energetic – the decision was hers.

Think "Nothing matters"

Next time you're aggravating yourself about whether to stay or leave, remember that worrying about the past or future is an utter waste of energy. Staying in internal and external reality is a way of reminding yourself that *nothing matters*. In the whole scheme of things – in terms of the world and universe – we are each just a speck of dust.

Someone once said to me, "That's all very well but you can't stop yourself worrying. I made myself ill because of a long drawn-out divorce that cost me a fortune." Well, he could have had a long drawn-out divorce without being ill. The illness didn't make the divorce any shorter or cheaper! Staying in the here and now puts problems into the right perspective. Rather than opt out, worry or be angry, you solve problems more rationally, more satisfactorily and you don't make yourself ill.

Say to yourself, "Is there anything I can do about this situation?" If there is, do it. If there isn't, stop wasting energy and focus on internal and external reality. If you're in a car in a traffic jam, for example, tell yourself things like, "I can feel the steering wheel against my hand. There is a red car in front of me. There's a policeman, waving his arms. I can see a blue car in the mirror. I can feel the seat against my legs and the pedals under my feet. I can feel my heart rate reducing. I am feeling calmer."

Every now and again, as your fantasies push their way into your consciousness, replace them with the words "Nothing matters". As you do this, you'll probably find that you take a deep breath. This is because, by cutting out the negative self-talk, you no longer view the situation as a threat. You reverse the physiological changes such as shallow breathing caused by your flight-or-fight reaction and you begin to relax.

Telling people to stop worrying doesn't help, but asking them to get into internal and external reality does. If you do this every day, you will begin to find that you catch yourself fantasizing in the car, in the bath, during a presentation, at your desk, at the airport. And you will begin to choose whether you act on the fantasy or stop wasting energy.

Practise controlling your thoughts, by staying in internal and external reality, as part of your everyday routine. To remind yourself to do this, put a red dot on: your mirror, your kettle and your rubbish bin.

Shaving, brushing your teeth, putting on make-up, making a coffee and taking out the rubbish are all things that you do on auto-pilot. And it's when you're on auto-pilot that your mind shifts to anxious thoughts about the past or future. The red dots will help introduce into your routine the skill of controlling your anxiety by staying in the here and now.

Learn from the tangled monkey that the more you struggle with obsessive thoughts, the more entangled in them you become. By staying in the here and now, you'll have a clear mind and a more realistic perspective and you will be able to make the decision that will ensure your life is a meaningful one.

Either make the decision to leave and resolve to act on it. Or stop fantasizing about your options, stay in the here and now and make the relationship work for you.

CHAPTER 14

HURDLE

4

Take responsibility
for your situation

(no blaming others)

Strengthen your will-power

You may be thinking, "Well, I've now learnt to control my thoughts and I've decided what I really want. So why am I still feeling unprepared to take the risk of living a meaningful life by crossing my Rubicon?"

The answer is that merely deciding we want something – in this case, to stay or leave – does not cause us to take the appropriate action. You still need to jump your fourth hurdle and learn how to take responsibility for your situation and stop blaming others.

In the past, you may have decided that you want to lose weight, meant it and yet continued to eat chocolate and other fattening food. You may have decided that you want to give up smoking, meant it and yet continued secretly to smoke cigarettes. As the philosopher Abraham Irving Melden says:

> "What a man *does* when he wants, is no evidence for his wanting."[1] [My italics]

Of course, wanting something may influence our behaviour but, when it comes to hard decisions, we often find that our will fails us.

I've worked with many clients who, time after time, promise me that *this* week they'll take action to make the changes to their relationship that they say they want. Yet the following week they come back with a million reasons why they couldn't do it.

Each time this happens, I completely identify with the psychotherapist Irving Yalom who describes his difficulty in mobilizing his clients' will, so that they will finally make the changes they say they want:

> "I sometimes think of the will, that responsible
> mover, as a turbine encased and concealed
> by ponderous layers of metal. I know that
> the vital moving part is lodged deep in the
> innards of the machine. Puzzled, I circle it. I
> try to affect it from a distance, by exhortation,
> by poking, tapping or incantation, by
> performing those rites that I have been led to
> believe will influence it. These rites require
> much patience and much blind faith." [2]

Maybe you identify with Yalom yourself each time you and your friends are stumped by your inability to summon the will to act. He goes on to say:

> "What is required is a more expedient, rational
> approach to the will." [3]

And a more expedient approach to accessing your will-power is to understand how you block action with your "internal resister". When you blame others for your situation, in many cases it is your internal conflict that's really to blame. Bringing unconscious conflict into consciousness and demolishing it will unshackle your will-power so that you are able to stick to your decision and get on with your life.

Be conscious of unconscious conflict

One of the most common internal resisters is Cautious You. Cautious You is constantly in conflict with Confident You and thereby undermining it. But who are Confident You and Cautious You?

Confident You thinks you can do anything with your life. This self is positive, encouraging, creative, a risk-taker. When it comes to leaving, Confident You says:

- "My possibilities are endless. I'll easily find someone new – and better for me."
- "It'll free me to get on with my ambitions. I can do anything with my life. It's now or never."
- "I must do what's right for me, not what's right for everyone else. Other people wouldn't want to think I'm unhappy and wasting my life just because they might disapprove of my decision. And anyway, in the end they'll come around."

Confident You is the source of your positive, uplifting, energizing self-talk.

Then Cautious You chips in with negative self-talk. Cautious You is hesitant, weak and apologetic and says things like:

- "Hang on a minute. What if I fail, what will people think?"
- "Without my partner, everyone will see me for who I am: a nonentity."
- "What if I never find someone new?"
- "I'm scared. I can't do everything alone. The finances, the children, the cleaning, the cooking. I'd better stay and put up with it."

And if it comes to staying, Confident You says:

- "I can change. It will just take some adjustment on my part."
- "I love my partner really. I can easily overlook the bad stuff and appreciate the good things."
- "Once we sort out our problems, we'll be great together."

And then Cautious You whispers:

- "The situation is hopeless. Nothing will change, no matter what I do. No one could try harder than I've already tried."
- "I can't try to change things now, it'll just upset everyone."
- "My partner just wants to control me. I can't fight it anymore. It's easier to just give in."

This is your inner conflict: the struggle between Confident You and Cautious You to take control.

When you're not conscious of this inner conflict, your thoughts vacillate between that part of you that wants to "fly" and believes you can do anything if you put your mind to it and the part of you that "nails your foot to the floor" by telling you that you are not up to it. This is when you suffer a crisis of confidence, become mixed up and unable to summon the will to stick to your decision.

Instead, you maintain the status quo and continue to live a mediocre existence with a mediocre relationship. Or, worse, you live an excruciatingly painful existence with an excruciatingly painful relationship, because you can see no way through the impasse.

Disempower Cautious You

If you become aware of, identify with and own both sides of your internal conflict – the inner voice of resistance versus the will that drives you to action – you will find that the conflict dissipates and you feel more balanced, decisive and confident about making your move.

To do this, have Confident You speak to Cautious You in a written dialogue. Let Confident You begin with the words, "I resent the fact that you ...". When Confident You has finished the point, write Cautious You's response. Keep this dialogue going until it comes to a natural conclusion.

Another way of doing this exercise is to sit opposite an empty chair. First, be Confident You and speak to your Cautious You, whom you imagine is sitting opposite in the empty chair. When Confident You has finished, get up and sit in Cautious You's chair and, as Cautious You, reply to Confident You. Keep swapping chairs as you continue your dialogue, until you feel the conflict between them begins to dissolve.

I realize this sounds silly but it's amazing how even my most cynical clients soon get into it and find the dialogue enlightening. Like them, you'll find the two extreme points of view quickly merge into a mutual understanding and you'll have clarity about what you really want and the way to achieve it.

HURDLE

5

Be aware that you always have a choice

(you're not as trapped as you think you are)

Change your name and move to California

Have I convinced you? Or are you still staying, "No, you're wrong. I can't choose to handle my life challenges, they're too overwhelming. I can't be authentic. I can't handle conflict with my partner, my parents, my children."

Or are you saying, "It's not that I care about upsetting other people. What paralyzes me is what needs to be done. I can't stay and:

- "Drop late-night socializing with friends."
- "Give up my lover."
- "Stop buying the latest gadgets."
- "Trust my partner not to waste more of my life with broken promises."

Alternatively, you may be saying, "I can't leave and:

- "Meet mortgage repayments alone."
- "Pick up the phone and ask for a job."
- "Take the first step to starting the business I dream about."
- "Face walking my children into a strange new school."
- "Live in a less desirable neighbourhood."
- "Face a solicitor and start divorce proceedings."
- "Tell my children that we're no longer going to live together as a family."
- "Attend my first dinner party alone."
- "Deal with the huge responsibility of being a single parent and sole provider."

To help you jump your fifth hurdle – to be aware that you always have a choice and that you're not as trapped as you think you are – the following technique may be valuable. I'll introduce it by telling you what I tell unconvinced clients who feel trapped by their stifling routine and weighty obligations:

> "You can do anything with your life. You
> can even change your name and move to
> California."

My clients' reply is predictable. They say something like, "I can't do that. I've got a partner and two kids to support."

"Well," I say, "you can put your two children in care and divorce your partner." At which my clients look horrified and respond, "I can't do that! I can't put my kids in care and divorce my partner."

I reply, "Yes, you can. People do both, don't they? So say the sentence using the words 'I *won't*' rather than 'I can't.'" After a little resistance, they try it and say, "I won't put my kids in care and divorce my partner."

It's remarkable how the atmosphere changes as my clients begin to realize that it is they themselves who keep them where they are in life. It's their own values that keep them doing whatever they thought they were being forced to do. No one's coercing them to support their family. They choose to. They want to.

Like Benoit's man who believes himself to be a prisoner trapped in a cell (see Chapter 6), once my clients let go of the glimmer of light in what's mainly a life of darkness, they turn around to see that their cell is of their own construction and that the door is in fact open. They can at any time, if they so choose, change their name and move to California. They are, and have always been, free.

On realizing this, many people choose to stay. Buoyed by their newfound sense of freedom, they decide to stay in a more genuine, involved way and to challenge and influence family decisions that impact them. In other words, to be more authentic.

Equally, if they've decided to leave, by changing their "can't" to "won't" – "I can't meet mortgage payments alone" to "I won't meet mortgage payments alone"; "I can't live in a less desirable neighbourhood" to "I won't live in a less desirable neighbourhood" – they see that they're *choosing* not to. They can, but they won't. They're not as trapped as they thought they were.

Stop hypnotizing yourself

You may still be saying, for example, "But I *am* trapped because I can't earn enough to keep myself and my two children."

To which, as an experiment, I'm going to say, "You could always live in a caravan and all go begging on the streets."

And you may well be horrified and answer, "I can't do that!"

Now try saying, "I *won't* do that. I won't have my family live in a caravan and go begging on the streets."

You could live in a caravan and beg on the streets. People do. What you're clarifying is that you choose not to, because neither living in a caravan nor begging fits with your aspirations and values. OK, so don't choose to live in a caravan and beg. But what do you choose?

- To find a job?
- To find a way to earn an adequate salary?
- To move to a less expensive home?
- To house-share?
- To have a lodger?
- To live abroad?
- To find a new partner?
- To borrow money?

Or

- To continue to tear yourself apart?

By saying "I can't", you're simply hypnotizing yourself with your own language. You must choose whether to stick with language that makes you feel powerless and trapped or to use language that will help you to jump this hurdle. Language that opens you to choices that may well create a less certain but more meaningful life.

Your choices have created your suffering, misery, frustration or discomfort. When you become aware that your hypnotic language is responsible for past and present beliefs about your lack of options, you can change your self-talk, feel more powerful and courageously take responsibility for choosing your future.

Paul was vacillating between staying with his girlfriend, June, or leaving for his lover, Jenny. He constantly said, "I can't leave June to fend for herself. She's not capable." Jenny was getting more and more frustrated and dealt with Paul angrily. Her anger was hiding her fear that Paul didn't really want to leave June.

Paul was torn between two uncomfortable relationships and blamed both women. When he began to stop saying, "I can't leave June" and instead said, "I can leave June but I won't", he realized that he was not as trapped as he imagined. He was in fact free to choose to leave June any time he wanted. He also recognized that staying in an unhappy relationship wasn't the best solution for June. The significant decision was not whether or not to leave, but how to leave.

Paul decided that he *could* leave, but in a collaborative way with an explicit contract that he would support June until she was on her feet and independent of him.

Change your language

To help you to take responsibility for your situation, instead of blaming others for it, and to help you make your choice, each time you find yourself using the following words:

- "I can't decide"
- "I can't stay and change our relationship"
- "I can't go and manage alone"

try replacing them with:

- "I won't decide"
- "I won't stay and change our relationship"
- "I won't go and manage alone".

Can you see how doing this impacts on how you feel? Once you were anxious; now you feel powerful, free to choose and to take responsibility for your choice. You have always been free to do anything with your life.

CHAPTER 16

HURDLE

6

Live by your own values and standards

(not everyone else's)

If you meet the Buddha on the road, kill him!

Even now, you may be asking, "Yes, Beverley, but how do I do it? How do I make my decision to stay or leave?"

If so, maybe you're continuing to expect an ultimate rescuer – in this case me! – to provide you with an instant solution, a panacea, a magic pill. You are still looking to an "expert" for direction, hankering after a solution to your dilemma upon which you can be sure you can depend.

Yet, as Sheldon Kopp, quoting the Zen masters, puts it:

> "'If you meet the Buddha on the road, kill him'.
> This admonition is saying that no meaning
> that comes from outside our selves is real.
> The only meaning in our lives is what we
> each bring to them. Killing the Buddha on
> the road means destroying the hope that
> anything outside of our selves can be our
> master. No one is any bigger than anyone
> else, there are no mothers or fathers for
> grown-ups, only sisters or brothers."[1]

"If you meet the Buddha on the road, kill him" is a mantra you must keep in your mind at all times, if you are to jump your sixth hurdle of living by your own values and standards (not everyone else's). There are no mothers and fathers out there for grown-ups, only brothers and sisters. Remember the 64-Million-Dollar Question, "Who has the answer?" (see Chapter 7) – and the answer that we make our own advice?

There is no absolute answer, no right or wrong, no higher authority to which you can turn. All you can be sure of is the ambiguity and anxiety that go with your awareness of total responsibility for one human life – your own. All you can do is act, evaluate and act again. *There is no right answer.*

Your job is to be you

You cannot continue to be forever trying to live up to other people's values, standards and expectations. Everyone has different attitudes, values and beliefs and so the expectations of others are not right or wrong, but simply *their* expectations. Your perfect is not my perfect. Your acceptable way of life may not be mine.

Right now many people love you because you're behaving like the good partner who follows convention and doesn't break rules, while others criticize you for living a lie. If you decide either to leave and break up the family, or to stay, demand change and in effect break up the family as it was, then those who now love you will be critical of you, yet those who are now critical of you will love you for being authentic. You can never get it right in everyone's eyes.

I've shown you some of the values and assumptions you may have adopted and taken for granted, such as:

- People must love and approve of me or I'll
  be miserable.
- Making mistakes is terrible.
- If I do something, I must do it perfectly.

And you have seen that these do not actually stand up to scrutiny and might even be unhelpful.

David and Thomas had been avoiding having their longed-for civil partnership ceremony so as not to upset David's parents. But David's attempts not to upset his parents, by conforming to their wishes, were instead upsetting Thomas. This caused a lot of argument, distress and distance between the couple. By the time I saw them, not only were David's asthma attacks increasing in number and strength but the stress was also threatening to break up their relationship.

When David's irrational beliefs about needing to be perfect in his parents' eyes were challenged, he was able to think more rationally. David realized that putting his parents' feelings and values first, and his own second, was not only making him ill but also making Thomas think that he was less important to David than David's parents. The obvious solution was for David to have the courage to be authentic. His parents have different values, attitudes and beliefs and that's OK. But he has to live his own life in his own way, if he's not to live a life of regret.

David and Thomas could either choose to change the situation – go ahead with the civil partnership – or change the way they viewed it – accept that the civil partnership was never going to happen. But it was pointless staying in the situation and viewing it with horror and distress. They chose to change the situation. David and Thomas had their civil partnership ceremony and together managed the fallout from David's parents, which brought the couple closer.

Had David and Thomas chosen to conform to the values of David's parents, to keep them happy, rather than to live their own values, it would have led to illness and a dysfunctional relationship.

By facing your unchallenged assumptions and questioning their validity, you free yourself to be more generous with yourself and respond more openly and creatively to life.

Make your own meaning

"Truth" is not an absolute but a process involving selection and interpretation based on our beliefs, knowledge, feelings and experiences. Have you ever been to a film and taken from it a message that seems meaningful and obvious? As you walk out in absorbed, stunned silence, your partner starts to describe a totally different and to you, banal, message. Isn't it incredibly annoying? But who is right? Or, at a dinner party you can see that a couple are obviously not getting along. Yet when you mention it to your partner on the way home, he or she is totally baffled by what you saw, not having noticed any disharmony at all.

Our understanding of our world does not come from outside ourselves but from our interpretation of events. The following situation, based on an idea conceived by the psychologists John D. Bransford and Merieta K. Johnson[2], illustrates this:

> "A woman was putting on her make-up in front of the mirror. She checked her outfit carefully and put the finishing touches to her hair. While she was eating breakfast, she read the newspaper and talked with her husband about where the family could go on holiday. Then she sent several emails. As she walked through the front door, she remembered that her son had been pestering her for a smartphone. The car didn't start. She got out, angrily slammed the door and ran back to get her bicycle. Now she was going to be late and dishevelled for her appointment."

Now re-read the passage using the word "politician" in place of "woman". And then re-read it with the word "unemployed" in front of the word "woman". How does your perception of the events change? What kind of newspaper was each woman reading? What tone did the discussions about the holiday have? How did each woman feel about her son's request for a phone? What did the house look like in each case and what type of car did each woman get into? What sort of appointment was she going to be late for?

Since everyone's interpretation of the same event will differ because of our different biases, beliefs, prejudices, past experience, intuition, knowledge and feelings at the time, the opinions, views and expectations of others can be viewed simply as hypotheses that are no better or worse than our own:

- Some think divorce is right in the eyes of God, others think it's wrong in the eyes of God.
- Some parents split up for the sake of the children while others stay together for the sake of the children.
- Some think it's morally superior to leave the partnership for their lover, others think it's morally superior to stay and keep their lover a secret.

Since there is no objective truth, no right or wrong, you must trust yourself and follow your heart. There is no meaning outside or independent of what you make of it. The reality is that there is no reality.

Do it – badly

Now you can stop being afraid of getting it "wrong". Positive action doesn't have to be perfect action. Waiting for the perfect way to leave or the perfect way to speak your mind can result in putting things off until tomorrow. So for all of you who are procrastinating because you're waiting until you can do it perfectly, it's worth remembering the inspiring words of G. K. Chesterton:

> "If a thing's worth doing,
> it's worth doing badly."

Instead of procrastinating because whichever choice you make – stay or leave – you want to do it "right", how about changing your mindset. Imagine crossing your Rubicon *badly*:

- Tell your partner what's bugging you *badly*.
- Broach the subject with your parents of your plan to divorce, *badly*.
- Leave *badly*.
- Pick up the phone and ask for work *badly*.
- Manage on your own *badly*.

Can you see how this takes the pressure off? Planning to "do things badly" can help you to stop procrastinating and to cross your Rubicon. Not only that: the chances are, by releasing yourself from the burden of perfection, you'll be more relaxed and logical. Consequently, you will be more likely to tell your partner what's on your mind *sensitively*, to broach the subject with your parents *agreeably*, to leave *decently*.

Do your own thing

You have to be true to yourself and live your life according to whatever defines what's right and wrong for you.

You hold back from asserting your own opinion, from contradicting others and from taking hold of your own life because you are afraid of your decision being unpopular. If you are to use your potential, you have to stop this self-image actualizing (see Chapter 9). Instead, if you are to self-actualize with no regrets, you need to hear the words of Fritz Perls in your head as you cross this Rubicon:

> "I do my thing and you do your thing,
>> I am not in this world to live up to your
>> expectations
>> And you are not in this world to live up to mine.
>> You Are You, And I Am I,
>> And if, by chance, we find each other, it's
>> beautiful.
>> If not, it can't be helped." [3]

Fully live your life

You may say that you would "do your thing" if only you could get back in touch with what it is you truly value. But so much water has flowed under the bridge since you knew who you were and what you wanted. Well now is the time to clarify which values will give your life meaning.

Since to choose is by definition an act of valuing one thing over another, each split-second choice that you make points to those values by which you wish to live your life: what you eat for breakfast, how much you smile, how pessimistic you are, how much alcohol you drink, whom you spend time with, how much you worry. Ask yourself what you are choosing and valuing now, and what you are going to choose and value from now on.

When it comes to the bigger question – finding your meaning and purpose in life – try asking yourself:

- What would I like my legacy to be? What would I like to tell my grandchildren I did during my life? What would I like to be known for?
- What would I like to have accomplished by the time I reach 94, in order to feel that my life has been productive and meaningful?
- Is there anything that I deeply value and yet feel I haven't fully experienced or realized in my life? What changes do I need to make and risks do I need to take, to more fully realize my most significant values?
- What would I like to do with my life if I could do whatever I truly wanted? (Assume, for the purpose of this question, that money is not a limitation – say you've won the lottery.)

In light of the above questions, write down what you need to accomplish if you're going to live a meaningful life and fulfil your purpose.

Consider what you'd do if you knew you only had six months – or 10 years – to live

Another way of clarifying your values is to ask yourself, "If I were told, God forbid, that I had only six months left to live, what would I do with the rest of my life?"

Well you'd certainly be clearer about what you valued and wanted; you'd be able to decide and act. If you chose to continue in your relationship you would no doubt be nothing but authentic, challenging and changing everything that bugs you. You wouldn't be worrying about the discomfort of a couple of evenings arguing.

And if you decided you value a life you cannot have within the relationship, you wouldn't hesitate at the thought of the temporary struggle to get back on your feet. You'd follow your head or heart. Either decision would be easy because you would have "nothing left to lose".

When you consider the prospect of having a mere six months left to live, it helps to put things into perspective, clarify your values and encourage you to do what's important to you, rather than getting it "right" in other people's eyes. However, most people answer the question, "What would you do if you had six months left to live?" with "I'd travel", which doesn't really help in terms of clarifying what to do with the rest of your life.

So try fantasizing about what you would do if you had 10 years left to live. Is the answer the same or different and, if different, how and why?

In the whole scheme of things, is it really so hard right now to go for what you value and live by your own standards? Are you going to continue to vacillate, to live with unfulfilled values and to respond to your situation by:

- Being bitter and cynical
- Daydreaming wistfully about what might have been
- Complaining that life isn't fair?

Or will you from now on:

- Gain the drive and determination to do something about it?

CHAPTER 17

YOUR JOB IS TO BE YOU

Move or improve

In this final chapter I want to summarize the core messages of the book. We've looked at how indecision is ruling your life. You persistently waver between remaining in your relationship and making improvements, or leaving and opening yourself to other options. We've also seen how your chronic procrastination leaves you constantly unsure of yourself, which is an uncomfortable place to be.

Any attempts to solve your indecision using conventional self-help methods – creating a personal vision, using rational problem-solving and brainstorming options, weighing pros and cons – have failed. And so has seeking advice from friends and relatives or help from professionals through counselling, self-development workshops and self-help books.

As few decisions are without any negative consequences, whenever you reach the point of resolution, doubt wriggles back into your mind and a host of counterarguments invade your head.

We've examined the paradox of how, by trying to avoid possible negative outcomes of a decision (discomfort, disruption or making a major mistake), you remain indecisive – and experience discomfort, disruption and the fear that you've made a major mistake!

Whatever it is that prevents you from making your decision – fear of upsetting others, of getting it wrong or of the unknown – you will never know what's right for you while you stay where you are.

It's time to move or improve. It's time to face up to those people who resist the change. It's time to live with the uncertainty and to meet the challenges head on.

Be authentic

You imagined that by doing nothing and remaining the same you'd get peace. We've examined how an "anything for peace" approach to your life means that you don't have to face the rows, the crying, the pleading, the unpleasant divorce proceedings or division of assets that go with splitting up. And that, yes, in the short term you do get peace. Yet, we've also explored how avoiding unpleasant scenes and tasks does not bring you peace in the long term.

You may try to convince yourself that living with dissatisfaction, or even the knowledge that things are dramatically wrong in your life, is not so bad. After all, perhaps an adequate home, relationship and job are the best that one can reasonably hope for in life, and we should all be glad of what we have. Everyone knows other people who are far worse off than themselves. Perhaps you should simply "pull yourself together" or "get over yourself".

This sort of thinking can get people through a few weeks, months or even, in some cases, years. But over time, by not being themselves and living their own values, they become bad imitations of themselves. If the unfulfilling situation continues, then the symptoms of dissatisfaction can become more extreme. Such people may start to have a problem with alcohol or drugs, become depressed or otherwise seriously ill.

How you live and make sense of your life is down to you. Although the support of others can be very helpful, you are ultimately alone. You must make your own decisions and deal with the consequences.

Be more selfish

I'm not advocating anarchy. What I am saying is that you have an obligation to be compassionate to y*ourself* as well as to others, to freely express your own views, choose your own path and take responsibility for the life you lead.

Michael worked in one of the Big Four accountancy firms. When I met him he had just come back from France, where he and his family had gone on holiday for the last five years. It turned out that he hated France and only went there to please his wife and children. At work, he had just been told that his boss did not feel he had the potential to become a senior partner, even though he'd spent years trying to be exactly what he thought the firm wanted him to be.

Michael was tearful and clearly depressed. He felt undervalued at home, had very little confidence at work and felt unable to be himself. He could turn to neither his boss nor his wife for support. Both seemed happy to exploit Michael's goodwill because, without effort, they were getting what they wanted. He also felt that his wife had turned his son against him by ridiculing the things that Michael valued, such as extreme sports and adventure holidays.

Michael paid a huge price both emotionally and professionally for not making clear his ideas and desires at home and at work. By grasping the philosophy explained in this book, he found the courage to give himself the same respect that he gave to others, and to be a little more selfish. He started to stand up for himself at home, insisting that holidays should be ones that he also enjoyed. At work, he started offering his own ideas and solutions rather than conforming to those of others, became more valuable to the firm and was soon seen as a potential candidate for senior partnership.

Choose life!

It is up to each of us to choose who we are and what we are going to be. There can be no blaming others. I have summed up this philosophy in the following three statements:

1. I am free

2. I make choices

3. I am responsible for my choices.

You are absolutely free to decide what you want to do with your life. You can't *avoid* choosing your way through life. You are personally accountable for all your free choices.

This new perspective makes it clear that you must learn to break free from the stress of inaction, escape your unjustifiable fears, cross your Rubicons and take positive action.

Many of my clients initially cannot stand the thought of living a life that is such an open-ended question. Maybe you, too, are feeling the weight of being responsible for who you are now and what you are to become. Yet, once you're here on this earth, your existence is what you make of it. In the words of psychologists James Coleman and Constance Hammen:

> "The youth who defiantly blurts out 'Well I
> didn't ask to be born' is stating a profound
> truth. But it is irrelevant. For whether he
> asked to be born or not, here he is in the
> world and answerable for one human life –
> his own."[1]

Rather than accept this, people choose to pretend that they can't escape the constraints of a conventional life – and by so doing remain caught in a web of self-deceit and blame. We've seen how you, too, may have been hypnotizing yourself with your own language. You'd convinced yourself that you can't stay and change things, and that you can't go and manage alone – or that you can't decide.

But we now know that the fact is:

- You *can* stay and change your relationship but you won't – you've chosen not to.
- You *can* go and manage alone but you won't – you've chosen not to.
- You *can* decide but you won't – you've chosen not to.

Define yourself

You are faced throughout your life with choices, some highly significant and others less so, but irrespective of their apparent significance you define yourself by the choices you make.

By choosing not to decide, you are responsible for the perplexed, vacillating, inauthentic, hesitant person you have become. Or maybe you've become inflexible, avoiding, resistant, aggressive, passive-aggressive, indifferent, depressed, desperate, opinionated or dowdy.

Previously you may have blamed others for the fact that you've changed over the past few years, and changed for the worse. But you now understand that you are in fact the sum of your choices. As Sartre put it: "I am my choices." So who are you on account

155

of your choices? Are you a bored housewife, an abused husband, an unfulfilled mother, a vacillating thirty-something?

Some of the fears that hold you back from taking action may be real. Most are imaginary. But, either way, the ultimate choice is between living a principled authentic life or a personally unfilled one. My wish is that reading this book is a defining moment in your life and that from now on you choose authenticity.

Be the you that you like

By accepting your responsibility for the person you have become, you become aware of the possibility of being someone different; the person you were before all this began or the person you always knew you could be. Someone who is collaborative, compassionate, courageous, self-actualizing, self-fulfilling, loving, sexual, ambitious, strong, caring, autonomous, authentic and decisive.

But to be disposed to collaborate, you must first *choose* collaboration. To be disposed to be honest, you must first *choose* honesty. To be disposed to courageously stick up for your rights, you must first *choose* courage. To be disposed to be decisive, you must first *choose* decisiveness.

A perspective on life that shows you that you are freely constantly choosing is one that also mobilizes you to take responsibility for the way you live your life. How will you choose to stay?

- Happily or begrudgingly?
- Empathically or angrily?
- Calmly or in a state of stress?
- With optimism or pessimism?
- With conviction or doubts?

Or choose to go?

- With enthusiasm or dread?
- Courageously or fearfully?
- Like a grown-up or a child?
- With care or indifferently?
- With conviction or doubts?

Be you and stay

From now on, each time you decide to follow your heart, plan to do it but don't, you know that rather than choose to cross your Rubicon and self-actualize, you've chosen to self-image actualize. And that's OK. But then you must let go of your dream of change.

You must stop complaining, accept the situation and be happy with it, because you know you've chosen it. You accept the lack of sex with your partner; accept your husband's unhelpfulness; accept your wife's irritability. Either change the situation or change the way you view it. There can be no blaming others.

If, on the other hand, you choose to stay and self-actualize, actively improving the situation, you need to cross the

Rubicon of raising the real issues, clarifying your expectations and agreeing how you'll live happily and authentically together. These expectations may range from trivial chores, like who puts the rubbish out, to major issues about starting a family, moving house or dramatically changing your lifestyle.

This may well involve managing conflict more skilfully by adhering to a new explicit contract. In this way, you are more likely to remain authentic and commit to and act upon collaborative solutions to problems.

Be you and leave

If it doesn't feel OK to stay, then you must self-actualize by crossing the Rubicon of leaving. This will no longer feel like such a difficult step because you now know that standing still in life is just as risky and stressful as moving on. Standing still is pointless, whereas moving on is self-fulfilling.

To be you and leave, you need to deal with your feelings of anxiety about your financial and social responsibilities or emotional stability. You may be anxious about telling your partner but, as you now know that changing your thinking can change your subsequent feelings and behaviour, you can either:

- Choose to feel anxious because you think you'll cause him or her pain, or
- Choose to feel angry because you still think your partner could have worked harder at the relationship, or

- Choose to feel indifferent because you think the situation is hopeless, or
- Choose to feel calm because you think that you can deal with whatever comes.

We've seen how one secret of taking the risk of crossing your Rubicon is to see your life as finite, as if you had only, say, six months to live. Because such questions put into sharp relief what's important to you, this sort of thinking can help you steel yourself before opening up a difficult conversation or making an unpopular announcement.

To live authentically – to be you and stay, or be you and leave – takes tremendous courage, but if you keep revving the engine with your foot on the brake, you know you're tearing yourself apart.

Be courageous

To find the courage to discover meaning in your life, Victor Frankl[2] recommends three different ways of living:

1. Through experiential values: by experiencing something or someone we value, such as a work of art, a natural wonder or being in love.

2. Through creative values: by being creatively involved in art, writing, music or invention.

3. Through attitudinal values: by having a good sense
   of humour, compassion, courage and, most of all,
   by finding the proper attitude toward dealing with
   suffering. If you can find meaning in suffering, then it
   can be endured with dignity.

Becoming conscious of your attitudinal values – the way you deal with the potential suffering that accompanies crossing your Rubicon – can help you make your decision and take the leap.

By having the courage to take the initiative, face up to your responsibilities and commit yourself to a course of action, you can engage with life and be your own person. My inspiration in moments of darkness, when filled with the anxiety of crossing Rubicons, has been the following:

> "To be a star
>
> You must shine
>
>   Your own light,
>
> Follow your own path
>
> And don't be afraid
>
>   Of the dark
>
> For that's when
>
>   Stars shine brightest!"[3]

The poem may seem a little twee on first reading but I put it on the wall above the phone in my office and every time I panicked or felt despair, I read it. The words helped me recognize that I was on my own and must muster the strength not to be afraid of the dark and just get on with it ("Just do it"), if I was to be the bright shining "star" I was meant to be! Either I could pick up the phone and take control or I could allow my circumstances to control my daughters and me.

No more "triumph of hope over experience"

We've seen how life is an ever-changing, ambiguous mixed bag and that no one's "truth" is any better than yours. There are no perfect solutions out there. You must build your own solution, your own life, customized to your individual needs. That takes time, effort, struggle, courage and determination. But until you accept this and are prepared to solve your own problems regarding your own life, nothing will change.

If you live in the hope that someone else will give you the answer, alleviate your suffering or grant you permission, like Kafka's man from the country, you'll wait for ever.

You must stop hoping that things will improve without your own energy, effort and pain. You can no longer sit at the crossroads and weigh up the pros and cons of your decision to stay or leave, hoping that both roads will merge into one.

You must stop obsessively talking about your relationship with other people, in the hope that someone, somewhere will have the key to your chains and make your decision easy for you.

You must stop allowing the "triumph of hope over experience". Let's deal with your experience and no longer merely live in hope. Let's once and for all accept that, in the end, you and you alone will make change happen.

No one can live your life for you, any more than anyone can die for you. You must live your life making your own meaning, just as you will die alone with your private thoughts, personal regrets and happy memories.

Risk making mistakes

By succumbing to your catastrophic fantasies and not taking a risk, you make your life miserable. As author Howard Figler puts it:

> "Risk is the tariff for leaving the land of predictable misery."

Zoe began to have serious doubts about her relationship in her mid-30s, after she had been with her partner, Theo, for four years. Theo was no longer interesting to be with, didn't want to socialize or go to the theatre, concerts, cinema and so on. Their sex life was virtually non-existent and he was resisting her wish to start a family.

Zoe's catastrophic fantasy was that leaving Theo could be a disastrous mistake. She feared that if she didn't meet anyone else soon, her biological clock might stop before she was able to conceive a baby. She would never have the children she yearned for. But equally she feared that if she stayed and Theo withheld making babies, she still might never have her family.

She "decided" on several occasions that she had no choice other than to leave and start dating again. Yet she would always come back to the possibility that perhaps he was the right man for her, he would eventually agree to start a family and so she should stay with him.

When I began seeing Zoe, her work had deteriorated to the extent that she was overlooked for promotion and her IBS and eczema were back. Zoe's thoughts were always coloured by the assumption that her risk lay in making a change, whereas if she wanted to avoid taking a risk, she should remain with Theo.

By working with me, she came to realize that, in fact, the risk of staying and hoping Theo would change was far greater (judging by past experience) than the risk of leaving and finding someone more compatible. Zoe left Theo and, within a year, had met Andrew who shared her dream of having a family. Five years later they were happily married, with two children. Zoe looks back on her decision to leave Theo as the best decision she ever made and proof that her catastrophic fantasies had been unfounded.

By taking the risk of making a mistake, Zoe was able to leave her "land of predictable misery".

Keep crossing your Rubicons forever

My perspective on life shows that you really have no choice but to live with the anxiety of crossing Rubicons if you are to find the right partner, achieve your potential and avoid stagnation. Living in a state of anxiety requires courage – the courage to address the promises you make to yourself at three o'clock in the morning, or while enjoying a drive along a sunny road, or while abroad on holiday.

The problem is that by the morning, by the time you've stopped the car or arrived back in the airport, in the absence of certainty about the outcome of your decision, back come your doubts and fears. You avoid taking action because of the anxiety created by the risks inherent in change.

While anxiety is both stressful and developmental, guilt is stressful and corrosive. The guilt you feel due to knowing you're not fulfilling your life is horrendous. To take the apparently safe path leads not only to pointlessness, but also to a sense of powerlessness, hopelessness, helplessness and quiet desperation.

You must choose whether to cling to the known and familiar fears or risk opening yourself up to a less certain but more challenging life. If you are to improve your circumstances and yourself, you must continuously go around the cycle of doing, reflecting, planning and experimenting in an upward spiral, as shown in Model 3.

Always learning, always changing, always improving, living your life to the full, doing what's right for you and others. But you'll never quite get there, since there is no end to

Model 3: Meeting the challenges on the way

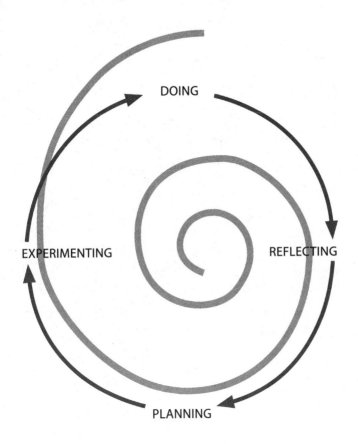

self-development. No one can afford to look in the mirror and say "Today I'm perfect – I never want to be any different than I am today. I never want anything different than what I have today. I never need to change."

For those of you who've been vacillating because you feel your life is somehow unfair, unjust or messed up by others, it's good to remember that:

> "Life is not about getting what you want; it's
> about meeting the challenges on the way."[4]

If you're to avoid living a life of regret, your decision to stay with improvements or leave with dignity must now be made. Your life must be about courageously meeting your challenges head on, by crossing your Rubicons forever.

Define the moment

To live life fully is, as philosopher Robert Pirsig advocates, to continually experience your existence at the "cutting edge of time".[5] The most dynamic approach to life is to define each moment; to welcome and jump the Six Life-Changing Hurdles every day of your life:

1. Take the risk of being yourself.

2. Accept anxiety as a positive, fundamental human experience.

3. Make your one and only life a meaningful one.

4. Take responsibility rather than blaming others, the situation or "life" itself.

5. Remember that you always have a choice.

6. Clarify your values and live by them.

If you don't define *this* moment by crossing your Rubicon, then the moment will define you – as a passive vacillator.

Ask yourself:

Am I now going to live my life on the "cutting edge of time" or will I be looking for another ultimate rescuer tomorrow?

Will I be telling everyone that this book is a waste of time? Or am I going to have the courage to close the book, cross my Rubicon and begin my journey to move or improve *right now*?

Is this going to be my defining moment ...?

DEVELOP AN EXPLICIT CONTRACT

Start now to develop new ground-rules and an explicit contract with your partner. You can do this by each making two lists under the following headings:

- This is what I expect of you
- This is what you can expect of me

Then reveal your lists to each other. Go through each point and agree what you are prepared to:

- Keep
- Lose
- Negotiate.

Keep your lists somewhere you'll both see them, like on the fridge door. Incorporate a rule that reminds you to review regularly how you're doing against the agreed ground-rules. Tell each other how well you're sticking to your agreement or remind each other that one or both of you has slipped. Then agree how you'll stick to your contract in future.

Reviewing can be done on an ad hoc basis, but you could also agree that you'll revisit your contract on a regular basis, such as once a fortnight. Eventually, the requested and agreed behaviours will become so automatic that you no longer need to resort to a written list.

On the following pages you'll find an example of an explicit contract for staying and an example of an explicit contract for leaving.

Example of an explicit contract for staying

Partner One

This is what I expect of you:

☐ Have nights out together over the weekend

☐ Be romantic and surprise me sometimes

☐ Come home on time

☐ Do what you say you will, not say one thing and do another

☐ Appreciate me and accept that I may be right sometimes

This is what you can expect of me:

☐ Sex regularly

☐ Be fun to be around

☐ Start a family

☐ Be a good friend to you

☐ Look after you when you're ill

Partner Two

This is what I expect of you:

☐ Wash up

☐ Sex regularly

☐ Give me credit for what I do, not nag me about
what I don't do

☐ Accept me for who I am and was when you met me

☐ Build me up with friends, not knock me down

This is what you can expect of me:

☐ A romantic night out with you once a fortnight

☐ Being lazy on a Sunday

☐ Re-start Sunday football that I stopped when I met you

☐ Say what I mean, not what I think you want me to say

☐ Wash up

Example of an explicit contract for leaving

Partner One

This is what I expect of you:

☐ Not to make everything into an argument

☐ To be grown-up about this

☐ Not to involve the children

☐ Help to make sure we both keep our friends

This is what you can expect of me:

☐ Be supportive

☐ Not to use the children against you

☐ Make sure you're settled somewhere nice

☐ Unhook so that we no longer see each other

☐ Be generous when sharing out our things while getting back everything that my parents gave us

Partner Two

This is what I expect of you:

☐ Not to use the children as a pawn

☐ Understand how painful this is for me

☐ Help me look for a place to live that's up to our standards

☐ Don't badmouth me to our friends

This is what you can expect of me:

☐ Not to be vindictive

☐ Stay on friendly terms

☐ Not to show you how much pain this is causing

☐ Take the collection of CDs and DVDs I arrived with and those I've since added to my collection

REFERENCES

Dedication
1. Lyrics from "Already Gone" (1974) by the Eagles, a song about leaving a relationship
2. Zunin, Leonard, with Natalie Zunin, *Contact: The First Four Minutes*, Ballantine Books: New York, 1976

Introduction
1. Lyrics from "50 Ways to Leave Your Lover" (1975) by Paul Simon
2. e.e. cummings, "A Poet's Advice to Students", in *e.e. cummings, a Miscellany*, Argophile Press: New York, 1958

Chapter 1
1. Beckett, Samuel, *Waiting For Godot*, Faber and Faber: London, 1956

Chapter 3
1. Kafka, Franz, translated by John Williams, *The Trial*, Wordsworth Editions: Ware, 2008

Chapter 4
1. Wheelis, Allen, "Will and Psychoanalysis", *Journal of the American Psychoanalytic Association*, Volume 4, 1956

Chapter 6
1. Suzuki, Daisetz Teitaro, *Manual of Zen Buddhism*, Grove Press: New York, 1960

2. Benoit, Hubert, *Zen and the Psychology of Transformation*, Inner Traditions: Rochester, 1990

3. Kopp, Sheldon, *If You Meet the Buddha on the Road, Kill Him!*, Sheldon Press: London, 1972

4. Bierce, Ambrose, *The Devil's Dictionary*, 1911

5. Yalom, Irving D., *Existential Psychotherapy*, Basic Books: New York, 1980

Chapter 8

1. Perls, Frederick S., *Gestalt Therapy Verbatim*, Bantam Books: New York, 1971

Chapter 9

1. Perls, Frederick S., *ibid*

2. Morris, Van Cleve, *Existentialism in Education*, Harper & Row: New York, 1966

Chapter 11

1. Model 2 developed from the Thomas-Kilmann Conflict Mode Instrument (Tuxedo NY: Xicom, 1974; CPP, Inc., Mountain View, CA, 1999)

Chapter 12

1. Kierkegaard, Søren, *The Concept of Dread*, 1844.

2. Frankl, Victor E., *Man's Search for Meaning*, Rider: London, 2004 (new edition)

3. Zen metaphor in Kopp, Sheldon, *ibid*

Chapter 13

1. Ricard, Matthieu, *The Art of Meditation*, Atlantic Books: London, 2010

Chapter 14

1. Melden, Abraham Irving, *Free Action*, Routledge & Kegan Paul: London, 1961

2. Yalom, Irving D., *ibid*

3. Yalom, Irving D., *ibid*

Chapter 16

1. Kopp, Sheldon, *ibid*

2. Bransford, John D. and Johnson, Merieta K., "Consideration of Some Problems of Comprehension" in William G. Chase (ed.), *Visual Information Processing*, Academic Press: New York, 1973

3. Perls, Frederick S., *ibid*

Chapter 17

1. Coleman, James C. and Hammen, C.L., *Contemporary Psychology and Effective Behaviour*, Scott Foresman: Glen View Illinois, 1974

2. Frankl, Victor E., *ibid*

3. Unknown source

4. Stone, Beverley, *Confronting Company Politics*, Macmillan: Basingstoke, 1997

5. Pirsig, Robert, *Zen and the Art of Motorcycle Maintenance*, William Morrow: New York, 1974

PUBLISHER ACKNOWLEDGMENTS

The author and publishers would like to thank the following for permission to reproduce their copyright material. Every care has been taken to trace copyright owners, but if we have omitted anyone we apologize and will, if informed, make corrections in any future edition.

Page

v ALREADY GONE
Words and Music by JACK TEMPCHIN and ROBB STRANDLUND
© 1973 WB MUSIC CORP. and JAZZ BIRD MUSIC
All Rights Administered by WB MUSIC CORP.
All Rights Reserved   Used by Permission

1 from "50 Ways to Leave Your Lover" copyright © 1975 Paul Simon. Used by permission of the Publisher: Paul Simon Music.

17 from *Waiting for Godot* by Samuel Beckett, published by Faber and Faber, London. Copyright © 1956. Reprinted by permission of Faber and Faber Ltd.

34–6 from *The Trial* by Franz Kafka, translated by John Williams, published by Wordsworth Editions, Ware. Copyright © 2008.

39 from "Will and Psychoanalysis" by Allen Wheelis in the *Journal of the American Psychoanalytic Association*, Volume 4, 1956, published by Sage Publications. Copyright © 1956.

48 from *Manual of Zen Buddhism*, copyright © 1960 by D.T. Suzuki, published by Grove/Atlantic, New York. Used by permission of Grove/Atlantic, Inc.

53, 126 from *Existential Psychotherapy* by Irving D. Yalom, published by Basic Books, New York. Copyright © 1980.

106 from *Man's Search for Meaning: The Classic Tribute to Hope from the Holocaust* by Victor E. Frankl, published by Rider and Beacon Press. Copyright ©1959, 1962, 1984, 1992 by Viktor E. Frankl. Reprinted by permission of The Random House Group Ltd and Beacon Press, Boston.

125 from *Free Action* by Abraham Irving Melden, published by Routledge & Kegan Paul, London. Copyright ©1961.